# ONE PLUS ONE EQUALS THREE—
# PAIRING MAN / WOMAN STRENGTHS

*Role Models of Teamwork*

*Emerson Klees*

*The Role Models of Human Values Series*

*Friends of the Finger Lakes Publishing, Rochester, New York*

Friends of the Finger Lakes Publishing
P. O. Box 18131
Rochester, New York 14618

Library of Congress Catalog Card Number 98-92966

ISBN 1-891046-00-4

Printed in the United States of America
9 8 7 6 5 4 3 2 1

# The Role Models of Human Values Series

*"Example teaches better than precept. It is the best modeler of the character of men and women. To set a lofty example is the richest bequest a [person] can leave behind...."*

*S. Smiles*

The Role Models of Human Values Series provides examples of role models and of lives worthy of emulation. The human values depicted in this series include teamwork, entrepreneurship, perseverance, and determination. Role models are presented to the reader in biographical sketches that describe the environment within which these individuals strived and delineate their personal characteristics.

These biographical profiles illuminate how specific human values helped achievers reach their goals in life. Readers can glean helpful information from these examples to use in strengthening the human values that are so important to our success and happiness.

Each book in the series includes a prologue that highlights the factors that contributed to these achievers' success. Since we are all different and we operate in varied environments, all readers won't take away the same messages from these books. The objective of the series is to present material that is useful to everyone.

## PREFACE

*"Man has not yet reached his best. H'e never will until he walks the upward way side by side with woma.' Plato was right in his fancy that man and woman are merely halves of humanity, each requiring the qualities of the other in order to attain the highest character. Shakespeare understood it when he made his noblest women strong as men and his best men tender as women...."*

*Eugene V. Debs*

The authors of many books, magazine articles, and newspaper columns accentuate the differences between men and women. In this book, the differences are de-emphasized; the emphasis is on the ways that women and men can work together as a team. We gain in a working relationship by taking advantage of individual strengths and by complementing each other's weaknesses.

In recent years, we have been barraged by generalizations about the differences between women and men, including the following examples:

- Women rely more on intuition and sentiment than men, who are more practical and generally have greater mathematical ability.
- Women have less upper body strength than men but have greater dexterity.
- Women are more atuned to life as a journey, and men stress the destination because they are usually more goal-oriented.

- Women are considered to be controlled by the right side of the brain, which is more intuitive, spontaneous, and subjective; men are thought to be driven by the left side of the brain, which is more logical, rational, and objective.

Let's set aside this concentration on differences, which has a tendency to drive a wedge between the sexes. In his book *Fire in the Belly: On Being A Man,* Sam Keen comments on these dissimilarities:

> Manliness and womanliness are both defined by a process of decision and denial. Each gender is assigned half of the possible range of human virtues and vices.... We do not know what human beings would be like if encouraged to develop their intimate promise without the systematic crippling effect of the gender game. Every man and every woman is half of a crippled whole ... Pasting simplistic labels—"masculine," "feminine"—on the feelings and modes of perception and action is like trying to make people goose-step in orderly ranks. Good men and good women alike can be intuitive, reasonable, playful, wise, erotic, or loyal.[1]

The nine pairs of men and women profiled in this book provide outstanding examples of teamwork. The environment within which each of these man / woman teams strived and the personal characteristics that each partner brought to the relationship are described. The profiles illustrate how the relationship worked in ways that make us envious.

Biographies are provided of nine pairs of men and women

who persevered in maintaining a productive working relationship in spite of personal differences and occasional dissimilar priorities. The diverse areas of endeavor represented by these teams include the activist movement, the creative arts, the humanities, science and industry, religion, and royalty.

Eight of the nine teams are married couples. Librettists / lyricists / playwrights Betty Comden and Adolph Green are collaborators who are married but not to each other. These achievers enlighten us by their example and provide us with role models worthy of emulation, which is particularly important in a time that appears to be virtually devoid of heroes.

This book contains material about Antoinette Brown Blackwell and Samuel Blackwell and about Lucretia and James Mott reprinted from *The Women's Rights Movement and the Finger Lakes Region. One Plus One Equals Three—Pairing Man / Woman Strengths: Role Models of Teamwork* is the first book in The Role Models of Human Values Series.

# TABLE OF CONTENTS

**Page No.**

## List of Photographs

Back cover: Illustration of *Clasped Hands of the Brownings*
by Harriet Hosmer, 1853

Cover design by Dunn and Rice Design, Inc., Rochester, NY
Photographic consultant: C. S. Kenyon, Rochester, NY

# PROLOGUE

*"Neither sex, without some fertilization of the complementary characters of the other, is capable of the highest reaches of human endeavor."*

> *H. L. Mencken, "The Feminine Mind."*
> *In Defense of Women (1922).*

1

This book provides biographical sketches of man / woman teams that are outstanding examples of men and women working together successfully. Selected from 19th- and 20th-century history, these nine couples were chosen as the pairs from whom we can learn the most.

All nine teams provide us with examples of relationships worthy of emulation. Although the couples represent individuals with very different personalities, their relationships reveal common elements. Three of the teams exemplify not so much instances of role reversal as cases in which the woman is more outwardly dominant than the man: Lynn Fontanne and Alfred Lunt, Lucretia and James Mott, and Marie and Pierre Curie. Queen Victoria and Prince Albert were both strongwilled, and the other five couples include less dominant, but not subservient, women.

The individuals represented in all nine pairs display a willingness to place their priorities second to that of his or her partner for the common good. When we think of the importance of priorities in everyday living—our priorities as an individual versus those of our husband or wife, significant other, children, collaborator, coworkers, relatives, friends, and neighbors—this willingness to play second fiddle half of the time, or at least part of the time, assumes a significance greater than we would ordinarily give to it. In fact, it is one of the principal lessons to be learned from these achievers' relationships, and it contributes heavily to the synergy generated by them. Because of this synergy, their combined output is greater than 200 percent.

The biographies include examples of the factors that contribute to the success of these man / woman teams, including:

- Communicating effectively
- Offering encouragement and constructive criticism
- Supporting each other's career
- Recognizing the need for some separateness
- Sharing household responsibilities
- Having different interests—sharing common interests

**Communicating Effectively**

All nine of these pairs possessed considerable strength in communicating, but two of the couples displayed this ability to a marked degree. Actors Lynn Fontanne and Alfred Lunt were incredibly successful in discussing each other's performances to make improvements in their acting. They discussed changes to their current play while in rehearsal, at home, and in bed, until the last performance. Their ability to communicate was an important factor in making ongoing, incremental improvements to every play in which they performed.

Elizabeth Barrett and Robert Browning were another notable pair with a high degree of communicating ability. They wrote virtually daily letters to each other before they met, while they were courting, after their engagement, and up until their marriage. Robert's first letter to Elizabeth began with "I love your verses with all my heart, Miss Barrett" and concluded with "I do, as I say, love these books with all my heart—and I love you too." Elizabeth's classic opening lines in *Sonnets from the Portuguese,* "How do I love thee? Let me count the ways" were written for the man she loved after finding the love that she never expected.

After the Brownings married and moved to Italy, they continued to communicate successfully in their daily lives together. On the rare occasions when they were separated, they wrote to each other frequently. After Elizabeth's death, Robert commented, "How strange it will be to have no more letters."

## Offering Encouragement and Constructive Criticism

These two couples also provide excellent examples of one individual supporting the other and making suggestions to improve the other's career. Alfred Lunt had a low regard for his acting ability. Encouragement from Lynn Fontanne was important to him throughout their life on the stage.

Early in their careers, Alfred didn't like accepting criticism from Lynn. She was the more thick-skinned of the two. They overcame this difficulty, and both of them gave and accepted the other's criticism willingly and without any introductory words of conciliation. Both Lynn's and Alfred's recommendations for improvement of the other's acting helped them to polish their performances significantly as a play progressed.

When Elizabeth Barrett and Robert Browning were married, she was the more accomplished and popular poet of the two. She gave him advice on improving his poetry, and he was helpful in offering constructive criticism to her. Both were able to take their writing skills to a higher level with the help of the other.

Robert outlived Elizabeth by many years. Later in his life, his reputation as a poet increased considerably. The Brownings provide us with an example of two individuals whose work wouldn't have achieved the impact that it did without the contribution of the other.

## Complementing Each Other's Career

All nine of these pairs supported each other's career in major ways; however, the Gilbreths and the Curies provide us with two of the best examples of this support. Frank Gilbreth, motion study expert and consultant, concentrated upon the technical side of his specialty. His wife, Lillian Gilbreth, who earned a Ph.D. in psychology, provided the people side of their team.

Frank dealt with the subject of efficiency, and Lillian concentrated on the impact of change on the workers. Together they were a complete team. Individually, they lacked some of the key ingredients of success. Working as a team, they were extremely successful.

Marie and Pierre Curie are the ultimate example of a man and a woman complementing each other in the workplace. When they met, Pierre had already established a reputation as a scientist, and Marie was just beginning her research work. She was referred to him to obtain the use of laboratory space and equipment. His specialty was the study of crystals, but he dropped that work to collaborate with her in the effort that led to the discovery of radium. Early in her research, the importance of her work became obvious to both of them.

Marie didn't balk at the strenuous nature of their research. Often, she worked until she dropped. Pierre was the less driven of the two. Together, they were an incredible team who made significant scientific discoveries. Neither of them would've accomplished what they did together without the support of the other.

## Recognizing the Need for Some Separateness

Although Lynn Fontanne and Albert Lunt were together both at work and at home, they recognized the need for privacy and for solitude. They kept their finances separate and didn't open each other's mail. In their three-story townhouse in New York, Lynn practiced her lines on the third floor, and Albert practiced his on the first. When they were ready to practice their lines together, they met on the second floor.

At their home in Wisconsin, Lynn's hobbies were sewing and decorating. Alfred's hobbies were cooking and gardening. Socially, however, there was no separateness. The Lunts were unusual in that one never socialized without the other. All of their friends were mutual friends.

## Sharing Household Responsibilities

Antoinette Brown Blackwell expected Samuel Blackwell to share the household responsibilities with her when they married. Samuel supported her in her career but didn't help with the details of her professional work—in Antoinette's case, her duties as a minister—other than serving willingly as a sounding board.

Frequently, Antoinette was away delivering sermons or on the lyceum circuit giving speeches. On those occasions, Samuel was in charge of the household and their five daughters, with a servant to help when they could afford one. Antoinette became a prolific author. Again, Samuel looked out for the family to allow his wife to have the time and the solitude to write.

## Having Different Interests—Sharing Common Interests

Queen Victoria was very outgoing and expressive. She didn't have the repressed qualities for which the "Victorian era" came to be known. Her interests were dancing, games, the theatre, and, above all, a happy home life with her family. Prince Albert, on the other hand, had conservative tastes and was very reserved. He was serious, studious, and hard-working. Two of his main interests were riding in the countryside and participating in discussions with talented artists and philosophers.

The interests that Queen Victoria and Prince Albert shared were dancing, music, and riding. Initially, Albert had no interest in dancing; he began to dance to please his wife and eventually enjoyed it immensely. Similarly, Queen Victoria grew to enjoy discussions with the artists and philosophers that Albert invited to the palace.

When they were first married, the Queen was reluctant to allow the Prince to share in her responsibilities. As the Royal Consort, he was paid an annuity by the government. Prince

Albert began by reorganizing the management of Buckingham Palace, streamlining what had become an inefficient operation. When the couple began to have children, Queen Victoria realized that if anything happened to her, Prince Albert would be appointed regent and would perform her duties until the Prince of Wales was old enough to rule. She began to share her responsibilities with Prince Albert to prepare him for this contingency. He was extremely industrious in carrying out his duties.

Marie and Pierre Curie were remarkable in having no separate interests. At work, they both conducted experiments with radioactive material, and at home they shared the household duties. They spent much of their time reading and writing technical papers.

When they weren't working, they both enjoyed exploring the countryside by biking and hiking. Most important to them were activities with their children.

***

Many other man / woman pairs could have been selected to provide examples of teamwork between the sexes. Two other examples are movie actors Joanne Woodward and Paul Newman, and stage actors Jessica Tandy and Hume Cronyn. Other choices could have included teams with local or regional reputations. However, these man / woman teams provide us with outstanding role models illustrating the synergy of the complementary strengths of a man and a woman working together.

No one set of abilities or qualities ensures the continuing successful personal and working relationship of a team. Success depends on the personal characteristics of the individuals involved, their empathy for their partner, the environment within which they strive, and many other factors. The following biographies describe lives worthy of emulation to help us achieve the healthy balance that is a requirement of successful relationships.

Lynn Fontanne and Alfred Lunt
Courtesy George Eastman House

## Chapter 1

## LYNN FONTANNE AND ALFRED LUNT

*"They are strange and wonderful personalities—very difficult to understand until you realize that they are not two, but one personality. Each is the other's complement. Together they are marvelous, their artistry amazing. Apart, they are oddly ineffectual. Alfred, a vaguely wandering soul who looks at you like a lost dog who is afraid of being washed; Lynn—splendidly null, a sort of highly intellectual ice-maiden. Alfred's genius illuminates Lynn; Lynn's strong brain and well balanced judgment keep Alfred within bounds and bring him back to earth when he soars skyward. I love them both, but the Alfred-Lynn combination is the real person, not the component parts."[2]*

*W. Graham Robertson*

Lynn Fontanne and Alfred Lunt, generally considered the premier actor and actress on the stage during the 1920s, 1930s, and 1940s, were a finely-tuned acting team who complemented each other to an incredible degree. They strived for perfection and continued to improve a play until its final performance. Occasionally, they would have a disagreement during a rehearsal, but by the end of the performance they would walk away arm in arm.

Each was willing to appear in a play that showcased the other's talents, but was only a light vehicle to display his or her own acting ability. They were teamwork personified, and their acting genius continued to grow the longer they performed together. They spent twenty-four hours a day in each other's company—by choice—and were happily married for over fifty years.

Memories of the acting abilities of Lynn Fontanne and Alfred Lunt have begun to fade. Their last Broadway play was *The Visit* at the Lunt-Fontanne Theatre in 1958. Although the Lunts performed in many serious plays, such as *The Sea Gull, Taming of the Shrew,* and *The Visit*, they are remembered mainly as the sophisticated and witty antagonist and protagonist in comedies.

Fontanne and Lunt aren't well remembered because they acted only on the stage; they had little exposure in the electronic media. They made one motion picture together, *The Guardsman,* and then rejected all other offers to appear in films. They did limited radio performances, which usually were shortened versions of their plays, as a supplement to their stage productions. They didn't perform on television until he was sixty-five and she was seventy, and they were nearing retirement.

Some actors, such as Jason Robards, Jr., and George C. Scott, performed both in films and on the stage. Others—Tallulah Bankhead, Helen Hayes, and Mary Martin—performed principally on the stage but also appeared in films to keep their names in front of the public. Fontanne and Lunt performed in their plays to many audiences on the road, but they reached only a fraction of the audience that they could have reached in films. Both Fontanne and Lunt seemed to have been born to perform on the stage; neither of them considered any other career.

## Their Working Relationship

Fontanne and Lunt were always open with each other when offering constructive criticism of the other's acting; however, it was difficult at first. Fontanne saw an early performance of *The Intimate Strangers,* and Lunt asked her for comments on his performance. She said, "You worked too hard. Act being relaxed." Of this early criticism, Fontanne said, "He didn't like that at all." As they matured as actors, two of their real strengths were their mutual support and their critical suggestions about each other's acting—feedback that helped to improve their acting skills.

In an interview, Fontanne said, "We were two actors being perfectly honest with each other. To an outsider it might have sounded cruel. We didn't sound cruel to each other. It's just that we didn't have to bother with the 'now-darling-of-course-you're-the-most-marvelous-actor-in-the-world-but-there's-just-one-little-thing' beginning. We've always been pretty straight with each other."

Fontanne observed, "Over a long run, you lose your eye and you lose your ear. And I have to keep watch over him as he does over me ... And I think that is very possibly one of the reasons, if I might say so, for our success. I think that we are terrifically critical of each other. And we've learned, the both of us, to take it.... If [when I'm performing] I'm tired and it gets into my own voice—I hear about it from Alfred. Make no mistake, I hear about it."

Late in their careers, when they made a film from their successful stage play, *The Guardsman,* an anecdote circulated about their comments to each other. After the second day of filming, the entire cast except Lunt, who was nervous about his performance, went to view the "rushes." Fontanne watched them, returned home, and declared to her husband, "I was awful. I don't see how I can go on with the picture."

Alfred asked, "How was I?" Lynn replied, "You were charming. You looked handsome and your voice was splendid. You'll have to change your make-up because you look as though you don't have any lips. But me—I'm hopeless. I look too fat and my voice sounds like an announcer at a rodeo, and my eyes are too small and I'm just so gawky." Alfred remained silent; he was deep in thought. Lynn exclaimed, "I tell you I can't go on. What'll I do Alfred?" Alfred said, "No lips, eh?"

In *Stagestruck*, Maurice Zolotow wrote, "It took about eight years after Lynn and Alfred were married until they fused into one being, until they were no longer Lunt and Fontanne, but the Lunts; yet the Lunt and Fontanne remained, separate personalities in the one being. They retained certain temperamental differences and sometimes these differences clashed so violently it seemed as if the Lunts would be split in two."

Fontanne was more stable than Lunt, who was vulnerable and continually doubted his abilities as an actor—even after he was highly successful. Frequently, Fontanne would have to jolt him out of his self-doubt with a comment such as, "Oh, Alfred, do stop looking like a horse in a fire."

On one occasion, Fontanne was unwilling to slap her husband hard enough to be realistic. In *At Mrs. Beams,* a light British comedy, Lynn and Alfred were called upon in their roles to have a battle royal on the stage. She tries to punch him, but he backs away. She wrestles with him and pushes him over in a chair. They roll over and over on the floor with each swinging at the other. The fight scene ends with Fontanne slapping Lunt "hard in the face," but she couldn't bring herself to hit him hard enough.

One afternoon in rehearsal, Lunt pushed his wife away and said, "Goddamit, Lynn, you are the rottenest actress I ever worked with." He turned and walked away, but she grabbed him by the shoulder, turned him around, and slapped him across the mouth so hard that his head tilted. Then Alfred folded his arms, smiled, and said, "That's more like it." Lynn responded, "Alfred, darling, sometimes I think you are a cold-blooded SOB." Lunt replied, "Sometimes, I agree with you."

The final version of the fight scene, which lasted twenty minutes, was so realistic that many in the audience gasped. Some theatre-goers returned a second and a third time just to see the fight. The Arctic explorer Vilhjalmur Stefansson saw the play forty-two times.

All of the Lunts' arguments were about acting technique. None of their friends could remember a time, either in their apartment in New York or at their home in Genesee Depot, Wisconsin, when they argued about a personal matter. Noel Coward described a difference of opinion when they were performing in *Design for Living*. "She went up on a line and she refused to admit that she had forgotten it, and she said that Alfred had thrown her off by changing his movements." Fontanne asked Lunt, "Are you going to put down that glass there?" He responded, "I've always put that glass there." She said, "No, you haven't. You put it down here. You're doing it purposely."

The argument elevated to the point at which Coward felt that they were "going to tear each other to shreds." Coward thought that the play would be closed. However, the Lunts realized that they were behaving unprofessionally and immediately ended their argument. Coward observed that after the rehearsal, "They [walked] out arm in arm as if nothing had happened."

At one point in their career, the Lunts owned a triplex on East 63rd Street. The dining room was on the first floor, the bedrooms were on the second floor, and the living room-studio was on the third floor. When memorizing their lines for a new play, Lynn worked on the third floor, and Alfred toiled on the first floor. Each spoke his or her lines loudly without disturbing the other. When they were comfortable with their lines, they sat in the same room on wooden chairs with their knees interlocking. They looked into each other's eyes and spoke their lines. When one of them hesitated or spoke the dialogue incorrectly, the other tightened his or her knees together, and they started over.

On one occasion, director Lawrence Langer asked an actor and an actress in rehearsal to give the scene the same attention to detail that the Lunts would give to it. The actress erupted, "How can any other actors expect to play together as well as Alfred and Lynn? They rehearse in bed!" She was right. Lunt once admitted, "Miss Fontanne and I rehearse all the time. Even after we leave the theatre, we rehearse. We sleep in the same bed. We have a script in our hands when we go to bed."

Fontanne was known for her youthful beauty; she didn't seem to age. Her movements were graceful, and her voice was sultry. Lawrence Lader wrote about her when she was sixty-one, "The real source of her beauty comes from inside. It seems to bubble out inexhaustibly, expressing itself in a dozen ways, such as the saucy tilt of her chin or the way she shows off a new gown like a schoolgirl."

Fontanne's sister Antoinette thought that the explanation for the transformation of Lynn from a plain-looking woman to a beautiful woman was "the appreciation of Alfred." Antoinette sincerely believed that Alfred recognized Lynn's beauty long before anyone else did. She was convinced that Lynn's view of herself was completely changed when she looked at herself through Alfred's eyes.

Fontanne and Lunt often played married or unmarried lovers who fought with each other verbally, physically, or both. Their humor was risqué and sophisticated. The audiences of the 1920s were less tolerant of overt sexual behavior and language than audiences of the 1960s and later. Fontanne and Lunt could get away with erotic love scenes because they were stylish, and because the audience knew that they were married.

In one performance, Lunt lay exhausted on a couch with his legs on Fontanne's lap. As Lunt described it later: "And suddenly, she ran her hand up inside my trouser leg. The audience was delighted with the business and so was I. And we just kept on doing it for a couple of years."

Lunt had definite opinions on roles involving good-natured love scenes on the stage. He said that audiences in the 1960s had reached a point of not enjoying sexual byplay on the stage because:

> Some recent playwrights have made sex a dreadful thing. Sex doesn't have to be ghastly. Sex can be most enjoyable. Lynn and I did morally outrageous things on the stage, and we enjoyed it, and the audience enjoyed it because it was gracious and lovely; and most persons have known the happy experience of sex, in

marriage usually, as Lynn and I have, but when when one plays comedy, naturally, there is going to have to be a plot and this means there will be some sexual intrigue and infidelity, but it is always in the spirit of pleasure not of tragedy.[3]

During one performance of *Caprice,* one of their love scenes was so steamy that an elderly matron began to squirm and made a move to leave her seat and the theatre. Her companion, another respectable older woman, took her by the arm urging her to stay while whispering, "Isn't is nice, my dear, to know that they really are married."

Lunt and Fontanne developed a technique in which they dovetailed their lines; although they delivered their lines virtually simultaneously, both were clearly heard. They first used the technique in *The Guardsman* and improved it in *Caprice* and *The Second Man.* Perfecting it required considerable practice; they could use the technique without the audience missing a word. The one speaking would break up a line at a breathing rest; the one interrupting would come in at that point while the initial speaker continued talking but in a lower pitch. Sidney Greenstreet was the only other actor who could use this technique in performing with them.

## Lynn's Early Life in England

Lynn Fontanne was born on December 6, 1887, in Essex, England, the third of four daughters of Jules Pierre Antoine Fontanne and Ellen Thornley Fontanne. Jules Fontanne was a designer of printing type.

As a young girl, Lynn memorized Shakespearean monologues, which she recited to her father's friends. Even then,
she had a strong voice. Lynn's sister, Antoinette, remembered
that "it could ring out like a bell in a room full of people when
she was little." Lynn's father took her to see *The Merchant of
Venice* with Ellen Terry and Henry Irving. Lynn stood in the
gallery and gave the "quality of mercy" speech along with
Miss Terry until "papa forcibly sat me down and made me be
quiet." Lynn remembered that "I was a very noisy, happy, and
exuberant child until I was eight, and it was then that my
mother scolded me for being clumsy and I got to be self-con-
scious and lost all confidence in myself." Lynn's sisters
became salesgirls and secretaries, but her only ambition was
to be an actress. She recalled that "I was thought by my family to be a talented actress from the moment I was born, and
nobody thought of any other destiny for me." A friend of
Lynn's mother knew Ellen Terry and arranged an appointment
for Lynn to ask the distinguished actress to give her lessons.

In September 1905, Lynn met the actress at Miss Terry's
home in Chelsea. Miss Terry asked Lynn to recite for her.
Lynn gave Portia's speech from *The Merchant of Venice,*
"The quality of mercy is not strained. It droppeth as the gentle rain from heaven...." The actress was surprised at the
audacity of Lynn's choice of Shakespeare, but she was
impressed by what she heard. Miss Terry didn't charge Lynn
for the lessons; in fact, she gave the aspiring young actress ten
shillings a week spending money.

Miss Terry got Lynn into the chorus of *Cinderella* at the

Drury Lane Theatre and arranged a walk-on role for her in *Monsieur Beaucaire*. Then Miss Terry fell in love with a young American actor in *Captain Brassbound's Conversion* and sailed with him to the United States when the play went on tour. Miss Terry told Lynn, "That's all I'm going to be able to do for you. If I helped you any more, it wouldn't be good for your character, for each one runs his own race."

Lynn met the American actress, Laurette Taylor, in London and became her protégée. In 1915, Taylor returned to the United States and invited Fontanne to perform with her in New York. Lynn performed in many plays with Taylor and continued to improve her craft. John Corbin, drama critic of the New York *Times,* wrote about Fontanne in September 1918:

> That she has extraordinary powers of personality has been obvious from the beginning. It would be a brilliant scene indeed that her entrance did not lift and inspire. But such power tends to bring with it the reputation of being a one part actor; and in Miss Fontanne's case the tendency is increased by her stature and angularity, which renders impossible the obvious tricks of impersonation. But the truer art of character is a thing of the mind; and with each succeeding part it is more evident that Miss Fontanne possesses it in an unusual measure....[4]

### Alfred's Early Years
Alfred David Lunt, Jr., was born in Milwaukee, Wisconsin,

on August 19, 1892, the younger of two children of Alfred David Lunt, Sr., and Harriet Briggs Lunt. Alfred's father was a wealthy lumber merchant who died when Alfred was two years old. Before he was born, Alfred's sister, Inez, had died of pneumonia, which caused his mother to suffer a nervous breakdown. Harriet Lunt never recovered fully from her daughter's death. As a result, she became overprotective of her son.

Harriet Lunt, a graduate of Lawrence College, was teaching school when she met Alfred's father. She was a beautiful woman and an intellectual. Alfred inherited his *joie de vivre* from her. Her outlook on life was based on a line from Oscar Wilde that she quoted frequently, "I can do without the necessities of life—but I must have the luxuries." These luxuries included a palatial mansion on Grand Avenue in Milwaukee.

Harriet Lunt took her son to the Davidson Theatre to see his first play, *The Golden Horseshoe*, when he was three years old. At the age of six, Alfred started a scrapbook of his favorite actors and actresses. Pictures of Ellen Terry dominated the scrapbook. Harriet Lunt read the novels of Charles Dickens to Alfred until he was seven.

At the age of nine, Alfred's "Lunt's Stock Company" produced *Rip Van Winkle* at Lunt's Wisconsin Theatre in the Alexander family's attic across the street. Alfred was the general manager, the director, the star, and the set designer. While attending the Milwaukee School, he won the 27th annual declamation contest for reciting Wolsey's monologue from *Henry VIII.*

In 1899, Alfred's mother married Dr. Carl Sederholm, a sophisticated physician who spoke fluent Finnish, German, and Swedish. Harriet Lunt and Dr. Sederholm had three children, Karin, Louise, and Carl, Jr.

Dr. Sederholm loved the theatre and the opera, and he took his stepson to hear *Faust* when the Metropolitan Opera played in Chicago. Alfred respected his stepfather and wanted to be like him. In 1905, Alfred traveled with him to Finland, where the young man learned to speak Finnish and Swedish. In Helsinki, Alfred performed in an Ibsen play with an amateur theatrical group.

Unfortunately, Dr. Sederholm made some poor investments in copper stocks and lost the Lunt fortune. When he died in 1909, Harriet Lunt had to sell the Grand Avenue mansion. She supported the family by running a boarding house while Lunt went to college.

At Carroll College, Lunt was fortunate to enroll in an "oratory" course with May Nickell Rankin, professor of literary interpretation and dramatic literature. May Rankin had a passion for the theatre and regarded drama as "the most universal of the arts." She recognized Lunt's genius for drama and impressed on him the grandeur of the theatre. Most importantly, she convinced him that he was a man with a mission—to act. May Rankin staged six productions a year, and Alfred starred in all of them. He also designed the sets and constructed the scenery.

In his junior year, Lunt transferred to May Rankin's alma mater, Emerson College of Oratory, in Boston. He acted at

Castle Square Theatre, which had one of the finest stock companies in the country at the time. On October 7, 1912, he debuted as the sheriff in *The Aviator*. He acted in six evening performances and a matinee every week and worked sixteen-hour days.

Lunt didn't make his broadway debut until he was twenty-five years old. On October 17, 1917, he opened in *Romance and Arabella*. Drama critics didn't give him rave reviews, but it was a respectable beginning. Reviewers said that he "did capital work," and that he was "notably good." The New York *Sun's* critic said that "Mr. Lunt has given us the most amusing character acting of the season."

## Lunt and Fontanne Meet

Fontanne and Lunt met in the late spring of 1919 at the New Amsterdam Theatre, when they both starred in the Tyler Stock Company production of *Made of Money*. Lunt was already on the stage when Fontanne arrived for the first rehearsal. She sat in the wings next to Sidney Toler, who later became popular in films as Charlie Chan. Fontanne watched and listened to Lunt on the stage and was impressed by his manner and his voice. Toler said, "That young man's voice is literally a gift from heaven. A voice like that can't be acquired. You have to be born with it."

Lunt had seen Fontanne a year and a half earlier in *Wooing of Eve* and considered her a fine actress; however, he hadn't thought about her in a romantic sense. As he hurried off the stage to meet his leading lady, he was captivated by her. He immediately became awkward and didn't know what to say. While attempting to impress Lynn, he made a sweeping bow and reached for her hand to kiss it. However, he was standing at the head of a short flight of stairs; he lost his balance and fell backward down the stairway. Playwright George S. Kaufman, who was known for his dry humor, later commented, "Well, he certainly fell for her."

Lunt wasn't injured in the fall. Later, he said "I was so exhilarated and happy as though I had been drinking champagne." Fontanne thought that the fall was "prophetic," both in terms of falling for each other, and because Lunt's confident manner masked shyness and uncertainty. Fontanne told actress Laurette Taylor that she was in love with Lunt, and Lunt confided to playwright Robert E. Sherwood that he was deeply in love with Fontanne.

When the Taylor Company moved to Washington, D.C., for the opening of *Made of Money,* Fontanne and Lunt spent every waking moment together and often took long rides in Rock Creek Park. Both received excellent reviews for their performances. Fontanne's reviews were more glowing than Lunt's; at this stage of their careers, her craft was more developed than his.

## Lynn's and Alfred's Courting Problems

Lunt's mother wasn't convinced that Fontanne was the right woman for her son. Harriet Sederholm visited Alfred in New York to restate her reservations while Lynn was on tour. When Fontanne returned to New York, Lunt was torn between loyalty to his mother and his love for Lynn. Alfred and Lynn argued about his mother's influence over him, and he went to Philadelphia to escape from his concerns in New York.

Fontanne asked Laurette Taylor for advice. About Lynn, Taylor said, "a more miserable pup you never saw." Taylor thought that the situation was serious and advised her to track down Alfred in Philadelphia to resolve their disagreement. Lynn went there; Alfred was pleased and relieved to see her. They patched up their differences, and Alfred said that he wouldn't let his mother come between them.

When they returned to New York, their relationship cooled down again. Taylor didn't know what had happened, but she noticed that Lynn "seemed doubly hurt. One difference was that she no longer wanted to talk about Alfred. In fact you could imagine that no such person as Mr. Lunt had ever met Miss Fontanne." This time, Taylor advised Lynn to forget Alfred and to find someone else. When Lunt's mother returned to Wisconsin, he telephoned Fontanne to ask her forgiveness. They went out to dinner and reconciled their differences.

Lynn remembered that dinner. "What a day that was. My, but we had a high old dinner together celebrating, and we were so happy. I didn't think I'd ever be that happy again. I didn't care if I ever acted in another play again. Just having Alfred back in my arms was all I wanted."

In 1919, Lunt played in *Clarence*. The five female characters all loved the hero of the play. The plot was true offstage as well; the five actresses who played the women's parts all loved Alfred. Nineteen-year-old Helen Hayes was one of the five actresses. Hayes' mother knew that Helen "was carrying a secret passion in her heart for Alfred." Helen was "certain this bony, brazen woman [Fontanne] was not for him" and wondered when he would extricate himself from this "sophisticated hussy."

Each night after the curtain closing of *Clarence*, Lynn strolled into Alfred's dressing room and stayed there while he dressed. Then, arm in arm, they left the theatre. Actress Mary Boland thought it "most unseemly for a single female to be going into Alfred's dressing room." Later, Boland attempted to talk Lunt out of marrying Fontanne.

Helen Hayes had even stronger feelings about Lynn than Boland did. To her, Fontanne was "Eliza Doolittle come to life ... Seldom have I seen a more awkward, skinny creature ... I squirmed with jealousy and resented her fiercely. I derived some satisfaction from knowing the cast felt she tried to impress us as she paraded in front of our hostile eyes." Years later, Lynn admitted, "I could feel it you know; I could feel the daggers right between my shoulder blades."

Hayes was in love with Alfred for several years, until she met playwright Charles MacArthur at a party. MacArthur, who had not yet met Hayes, saw her across the room. He walked over to her, offered her a bowl of salted peanuts, and said, "I wish these were emeralds." Hayes had met the man of her dreams, and it was easy for her to forget Alfred. Subsequently, Hayes and MacArthur were married.

## The Lunt / Fontanne Marriage

Lunt and Fontanne moved into a theatrical boarding house on west 70th street. Lynn had a suite on the third floor, and Alfred had a room in the basement. It was a romantic time for them. They strolled in Central Park, rode the doubledecker buses on Fifth Avenue, and watched the ships in New York harbor from a bench in Battery Park. Playwright Noel Coward came to New York from London and visited them in the brownstone on 70th street. Later, Coward remembered the plans that they had made:

> From these shabby, congenial rooms, we projected ourselves into future eminence.... Lynn and Alfred were to be married. That was the first plan. Then they were to become definitely idols of the public. That was the second plan. Then this all successfully accomplished, they were to act exclusively together. This was the third plan. It remained for me to supply the fourth, which was that when all three of us had become stars of sufficient magnitude to be able to count upon an individual following irrespective of each other, then, poised serenely upon that enviable plane of achievement, we would meet and act triumphantly together.[5]

Fontanne and Lunt succeeded with the plan that they had made with Noel Coward when they were young. Early in their careers, they performed in separate plays, frequently in different cities. Then they insisted on at least performing in the same city. When they had achieved stardom, they only performed together. This was possible because they were the most successful actress and actor performing for the Theatre Guild. The Theatre Guild could guarantee a play's success by including the Lunts in the cast. The final phase of the plan that they made with Coward was implemented when they appeared in his plays beginning with *Design for Living.*

Fontanne and Lunt set May 27, 1922, as their wedding date. On the morning of the 26th, Lunt became impatient. They were sitting on a bench in Central Park when he said, on the spur of the moment, "Let's get married! Now! Immediately!" Since the wedding was to be a small civil wedding anyway, he asked her why they should wait another day.

They took the subway to City Hall and asked who could marry them. Deputy City Clerk James J. McCormick agreed to perform the ceremony and asked where their witnesses were. Two employees from the city clerk's office agreed to serve as witnesses in the chapel of the Municipal Building. An embarrassed Fontanne and Lunt realized that they had no money with them to pay for the wedding license. They borrowed the $2.00 fee from the witnesses.

Lynn and Alfred had delayed getting married for economic reasons. Lunt had been sending money home to help his mother with the expenses of raising his stepsisters and stepbrother. After he and Lynn were married, he sent a telegram to his mother: "Have made an honest woman of Lynn."

Fontanne and Lunt went on a short honeymoon to Atlantic City. Their friend, Billie Burke, was so upset that none of their friends had attended their wedding that she offered to arrange a church wedding. The recently-married couple had a second wedding ceremony to please their friends.

Later in life, the Lunts used a short piece of repartee when they were being honored and in interviews:

> He: In all our years together there has never been one thought of divorce.
> She: Oh, no, never.
> He: Murder, yes!
> She: Yes!
> He: But never divorce.

Their support for each other was evident to all of their friends and colleagues in the theatre. In his biography, *The Fabulous Lunts,* Jared Brown shared his thoughts:

> Many married couples become more dependent upon one another as they grow older and their friends pass away, but the Lunts' mutual reliance dated from the beginning of their relationship. Seldom have two people been so interdependent, so genuinely in harmony. From the very beginning of their married life, they shared a mutual respect and affection that grew stronger through the years. At first their reliance on one another seems to have been primarily related to their work. Each realized that the other was his best critic, and each depended on the other for advice.[6]

Fontanne and Lunt did everything together; they weren't comfortable when apart. In 1930, Alfred went for a walk alone and stopped to visit a friend for about a half hour. It was just before dinnertime, and the friend asked Alfred if he would like to go out to dinner with him. Alfred was aghast. "Without Lynn?" he asked. He grabbed his hat and hurried home.

Alexander Woolcott, author and theatre critic, became a close friend of the Lunts. He never married, and he didn't have a high opinion of the institution of marriage. He invited either a husband or a wife to his dinner parties, but not both. His married friends didn't like this arrangement, but they went along with it. However, the Lunts refused. If he wanted Lynn at his dinner party, he would have to tolerate the presence of Alfred, and vice versa. Woolcott ranted and raved but complied with their wishes. He later admitted that they were better as a couple than they were separately; they were the exception to his rule.

Noel Coward had learned this about Lynn and Alfred early in their friendship. Initially, Coward tried to determine whether he enjoyed the company of one more than the other. One day he experienced an epiphany—Lynn and Alfred weren't two separate people. Coward said, "They were one person and now I realized why I'd never been able to decide between them."

In the mid-1960s, their friend, Alan Hewitt, experienced an example of their closeness.

> Alfred called me around 6:30 or 7:30 in the evening and said, "Are you doing anything for dinner?" and I said, "Well, I was just going about to fix something for myself here." He said, "Would you do me a great favor? We've got so much food here, and I'd like you to help

me with it. Lynn has fallen and broken her arm you see, and I've taken her to Doctor's Hospital. So we have all of this perfectly good food here, and she's not here to eat it. Would you come up and share it with me?" So I said, "Of course." And so I went up to have dinner with him.

Alfred offered me a drink, and then said, "Now, before we have dinner, if you don't mind, I'm just going to run over and see Lynn." So he went over to Doctor's Hospital, which was just a block away. When he came back, the cook served dinner, and before dessert Alfred said, "I'm sorry, Alan, but I've got to make sure that Lynn's all right. You don't mind, do you?" And back he went to the hospital. Well, that evening, he went there four times! And as I was leaving, he said, "Why don't I walk part of the way with you? It'll give me a chance to stop at the hospital and see how Lynn is doing."[7]

Fontanne surprised her English friends on one occasion with her response to an invitation. Lady Juliet Duff asked Fontanne to have lunch with her and Lady Cynthia Asquith. Lynn replied, "I couldn't, I'm afraid, unless you ask Alfred too. I don't go anywhere without him." The ultimate anecdote about their togetherness involved the time that Lynn was asked by the Duchess of Windsor, "Is it true that you and your husband sleep in separate bedrooms?" Lynn replied, "Alfred and I don't even sleep in separate beds."

One reason for their closeness was that they didn't have

the usual division between their work and their personal lives. They experienced everything together. Noel Coward often wondered whether they acted so well together because they loved each other so much, of if they loved each other so much because they acted so well together. He observed, "Sometimes I've thought that they are in the theatre so intensely because the theatre makes it possible for them to be together more often and in more ways than they might be if they were in some other line of work."

When asked what had kept them together, Lynn answered that she remembered admiring Alfred's voice and acting technique the first time they met. She fell madly in love with him and was intoxicated with his presence from then on. Lynn concluded by saying, "I suppose it is rather unusual but there it is."

Alfred's response to the same question was, "People always want to know why we get on so well together and the answer is I've never been bored. She's the most exciting person I've ever known, and I'm in love with her. Married life is spending all your time with a charming person who makes life more interesting because you can spend so much time with her."

Fontanne was asked about the basis of the strength of their marriage. She replied that a mutual respect for each other's privacy was the foundation. She added:

> I think we're an utter necessity for each other. Neither Alfred nor I dislikes solitude. We like each other's company, but we also cherish our

own privacy. We can both be here in the house together and yet not be side by side, just aware of our presences. Alfred can be in the garden all morning while I'm going about my own affairs.... Neither Alfred nor I is possessive. Nor do we take from the other. We're incurious about the other's privacy. We don't open each other's mail. We have our own bank accounts. We split all house expenses and we each pay for our own clothes and medicines and doctors and I pay for my own maid. Consequently, we don't have any serious arguments over money.[8]

On their twenty-eighth wedding anniversary, the Lunts were asked how they had remained happily married for nearly thirty years. They replied:

We always have been careful to separate our personal and our professional lives. We are together practically all the time offstage; once we enter the stagedoor we are like polite strangers. There is no visiting between dressing rooms. We have work to do until the curtain falls at eleven o'clock. After that we always resume our other life and generally go straight home....

When we spend our summer holidays on our farm in Wisconsin, we are careful to give each other plenty of time to be alone to devote to separate interests [decorating and sewing for her, cooking and gardening for him]. On the other hand, we are fortunate also in liking the same people, so that our friends are always mutually welcome. Neither of us is much of a partygoer. Many of our friends are outside the theatre as well as in it. We like nothing better than having a quiet dinner together, and we never have come to that unfortunate state in which you "run out of conversation" which sometimes happens to people who have been married a quarter of a century.[9]

Because of their closeness, the Lunts' friends were worried about the surviving partner when one of them died. They were particularly concerned if Alfred outlived Lynn; they considered him much less able to handle the grief. Alfred passed away on July 21, 1977; Lynn died in her sleep on July 30, 1983. Several years after Alfred's death, an interviewer asked Lynn, "With all the triumphs and accolades you've received through the decades, what was the real highlight?" Without hesitation, Lynn replied, "My marriage to Alfred—I miss him every second of every day."

Adolph Green and Betty Comden
Courtesy University of Southern California
Department of Special Collections

## Chapter 2

## BETTY COMDEN AND ADOLPH GREEN

*"... perhaps the greatest wonder is the joint career of Betty Comden and Adolph Green, merry-andrews and collaborators extraordinary. For twenty-two years, Comden and Green have amicably and successfully collaborated as performers with other performers; as lyricists with several different composers, choreographers and librettists; as librettists with a half dozen directors and producers, as authors with a swarm of temperamental stars; and, needless to say, with each other. It is a record of harmony unique in the theatre."*[10]

*Peter Lyon in "The Antic Arts: Two Minds That Beat As One" in Holiday magazine, December 30, 1961.*

Betty Comden and Adolph Green collaborated on films, musicals, and revues for over fifty years. Neither has written a libretto, lyric, or screenplay without the other. They think as one person, and one is rarely mentioned without the other. In fact, they're treated as one person in their contracts. After over fifty years of collaboration, they have the ability to speak virtually as one person. One starts a sentence, and the other finishes it.

They seldomly disagree about their work. Their main personal difference is about being on time. Betty is always on time, and Adolph is usually late, although he has become more punctual as he has grown older. Betty is calm and under control, in contrast to Adolph, who is always restless and moving around. Betty has a vivid imagination, a strong sense of humor, and a sharp wit, which she rarely uses to be unkind. Adolph, who also has a brilliant imagination, has an encyclopedic mind and a zany, unpredictable sense of humor. Their personal strengths are amazingly complementary. They've accomplished together what they couldn't have done alone.

Betty Comden and Adolph Green are known as the prolific librettists / lyricists for many Broadway musicals, including *On the Town, Wonderful Town, Bells Are Ringing, Do Re Mi, Fade Out—Fade In, Hallelujah,* and *Applause.* They are also known for writing screenplays and lyrics for movies, including *On the Town, Singin' in the Rain,* and *The Band Wagon.* They were the recipients of the Writers Guild Award for *On the Town,* 1949; *Singin' in the Rain,* 1952; and *Bells Are Ringing,* 1960.

**The Nature of Their Collaboration**

Betty Comden and Adolph Green began their collaboration in the late 1930s. Their first joint effort was in preparing material for the Revuers, a quintet of comedians and singers in which they performed at the Village Vanguard. They looked for material for their act and were told that they would have to pay royalties, which they couldn't afford. Betty and Adolph began to write all of the material for their acts, including music, lyrics, and skits.

Comden and Green worked every day, usually in Betty's apartment. They met about one o'clock and planned the day's work over a lunch of sandwiches and coffee. Initially, Betty captured their ideas with a pencil and a yellow legal pad. Later, she switched to a portable typewriter. Adolph described their methods: "Sometimes when you're on a project, you go all day and all evening. Sometimes you just work only a short time. It depends on what stage the project is in."

Writer Peter Lyon captured their different natures:

> Betty Comden and Adolph Green present an odd contrast ... She is carefully composed; he is tense, as though he had been wound up too tight. Her voice is soft and pitched low; his rises, excited and extravagant. She is murmurous; he is clamorous. Her manner is tentative and seems almost apologetic; his is offhand and abrupt. In repose, her mouth curves down, her expression sad and her face quite beautiful; even if his face were ever in repose, the same could scarcely be said of it.

> And yet, as they speak, the dissimilarities blur. Each refers to the other with a glance, with a grimace; each sets the other to chuckling; they are constantly attuned, it is clear, to the same wavelength.[11]

Betty says that "Adolph and I have lots of old, outdated references and phrases we have mutually piled up over the years. There is a kind of radar between us, knowing what the other is thinking based on stuff were have both read or shared." Betty tells a story about their being on the same wavelength that occurred on Adolph's thirty-third birthday. She met him in midtown Manhattan and noticed that he was subdued and even somewhat gloomy. She thought that he was probably depressed because he was thirty-three-years old and felt that he hadn't accomplished as much as he should've by this time.

Betty knew of a book, *At Thirty-three,* by Eva LeGalienne, the founder of the Civic Repertory Theatre, about her life up to that age. It wasn't a best-seller, but Betty, knowing that Adolph was a voracious reader, figured that he had probably read it. She turned to him and said, "Eva LeGalienne?" He nodded his head in agreement and continued walking. He knew exactly what she meant by the question. Anyone overhearing the interchange wouldn't have had an inkling of its meaning.

In *Off Stage,* Betty describes Adolph: "The mythic character of my life, my partner, Adolph Green, it seems to me must have sprung full-blown from his own head. There is no other head quite capable of having done the job. Only his head has the antic, manic imagination and offbeat creative erudite-plus childlike originality to conceive of such a person." She gives a lengthy example of how her collaborator creates, along with the comment, "I can just hear his head making him up."

> "How's about I jump out like this ... tall, blond, grand, and NAH!" The head shakes with fierce rejection. "How's about medium, dark, Hungarian, with a Hapsburg jaw and lots of assorted teeth ... and I'll study music and literature and the cinema and ... NAH!" Again the head shakes violently. "I'll just absorb it all, sort of osmosis-wise, simply by listening and reading and watching and just being, and I'll store it away in here along with stuff like the succession of the heavyweight boxing champions of the world, the famous old Yankee lineups, the great comic strips, and vaudeville acts and songs like 'I Wish That I Was Born in Borneo,' ... and my body will be like Michelangelo's David and—the head snorts dismissively—NAH!"

> "Who needs it? ... It will be spare and strong with a well-turned leg—two of them, in fact— and they will be able to lift me into the air like Nureyev, and I will have an easy rhythmic saunter like—dare I say it? What the hell!— like Astaire, so that some critic one day will write of me, 'A dancer of rare comedic grace,' and somewhere early on I'll meet a girl and we'll be on the same wavelength, and we will have a big career together with nary a thought

of romance, let alone marriage. And I'll have a nice voice like Placido, and ... NAH PLEASE! but it will be loud, very loud, but sometimes surprisingly tender and good on ballads, and I'll know acres and acres of poetry and miles and miles and miles of art, and I'll know every piece of music ever written, and I'll be able to sing it, replicating a full orchestra if need be, and I'll know the director and stars and cast, down to the last extra, of every movie ever made."

"And, listen, so I may get depressed once in a while *(once in a while!!!???),* but here comes the best part: I'll be funny. I'll be able to make people laugh. I'll be witty. I'll say things in an unexpected way, spontaneously juxtaposing odd thoughts and words, giving them a kind of surreal twist, and ... and ... NAH! that's not the best part. The best part is I'll marry the most beautiful, gifted girl in Jersey City and all the rest of the world and have two smashing children ... And wow! No one will believe such a creature could exist, but I *will!!!* I *will!!!* Here I come, ready or not!!!!!!!!!"[12]

Comden and Green place considerable emphasis on structure in writing the story for a musical or a screenplay. Adolph observes that "What we find most effective is structuring the book as much as we can before writing any songs. The more structure you have, the better off you are, and the more tightly the plot will mesh." They have been extremely successful incorporating the songs into the storyline, something that was not emphasized until they did it. Two of their early successes at doing this were *Singin' in the Rain* and *The Band Wagon.*

Betty adds: "That doesn't mean that you don't start working on the score before the book is written. People like Leonard Bernstein, Jule Styne, Cy Coleman are dramatists, and they always write for the theatre, for situation and character. It's collaborative, flexible." Comden and Green remember vividly the constantly changing approach used in creating *On the Town.* "Sometimes Leonard [Bernstein] had some melody that he decided should be used, and we put words to it. Other times we came with a full lyric, and he'd work on it. Still other times we'd have an idea and start working on it together. And we'd use patterns of other songs and start putting a few lines of lyric to them, just to get a start."

Comden and Green always used experiences from their own lives in their work. Early in their careers, they went to Hollywood, and the movie for which they were to write the screenplay was cancelled. They weren't able to find other work in Hollywood. Betty returned to New York first, and then Adolph returned because his mother was ill. Betty met him at Grand Central Station carrying a sign that read "The Adolph Green Fan Club" when he returned.

They used that idea in *The Band Wagon,* when Fred Astaire, playing an actor whose career was fading, walked slowly and dejectedly up the railroad station ramp singing "By Myself." He was met by two friends, played by Oscar Levant and Nanette Fabray, carrying "fan club" signs that cheered him up.

One of their hit songs was "Just in Time" from *Bells Are*

*Ringing* that starred Judy Holliday. Jule Styne wrote a simple melody for which no lyrics were written for several months. They referred to it as "Da-Da-Da." Finally, they found a situation in the storyline that provided them with the title, "Just In Time." Their creative process encompassed many variations on a theme. They were very pragmatic. If it worked, they used it.

Another technique they employed was to listen to the audience. Betty observed that: "You listen to what they're saying, not necessarily to the critics. We like the idea of going out of town. You have to listen to the audience, plus keep in mind what your own intention was."

On occasion, the collaborators encountered "second act trouble." Adolph commented on that phenomenon: "That's probably because the story isn't spreading itself out in inevitable fashion, which is what you strive for. Very often the problems are in the first act. The second act has to play off whatever you've set up in the first."

Because they've been so successful, the impression is sometimes given that it has been an easy road. Adolph describes the creative process as "agony." He explains their way of generating an idea. "Just read, think, kick around things, meet every day and stare at each other and say no to something for a year, then suddenly say, 'Let's try it.' Sometimes other people you're involved with get enthusiasm and pull you along, and suddenly you say, 'Well, this can work.'"

Comden and Green always collaborated with each other.

In careers that spanned over fifty-five years, neither of them worked with another collaborator. They were once asked if either of them had ever considered working on their own. They both quickly responded: "Never! Unthinkable!"

Betty has summed up the reasons for their success:

> We write with humor about basically serious things. We like to think we're expressing something of ourselves, something of what we feel is important in the world today. At the same time, we try to help audiences feel the way they should when they leave the theatre — that is, glad to be alive. That windows have been opened, fresh air has been let in, and they're leaving as happy people.[13]

They certainly accomplished their goal of making people — thousands of people — happy. It is difficult to imagine what the world of the Broadway musical and musical films would be like without the contributions of Comden and Green.

**Early Life and Career**

Betty Comden was born Betty Cohen on May 3, 1917, in Brooklyn, New York, to Leo and Rebecca Sadvoransky Cohen. Her first acting experience came at the age of eleven when she was cast as Rebecca in Sir Walter Scott's *Ivanhoe* in the seventh grade at the Brooklyn Ethical Cultural School. After graduating from Erasmus Hall High School, she majored in drama at New York University. She graduated with a B.S. degree in drama in 1938 and began acting in theatre groups.

Adolph Green was born on December 2, 1914, in the Bronx, New York, to Daniel and Helen Weiss Green. In grammar school, he wrote poetry and acted in plays. He grew up loving music, and, although he did not receive formal training in music, he developed an encyclopedic musical memory. In 1934, he graduated from DeWitt Clinton High School and attended college, but he didn't complete the courses required for a degree. During the day, he worked as a runner on Wall Street and then as an installer for a carpet company; in the evenings, he participated in little theatre groups.

Comden and Green met through a mutual friend while Betty was at New York University. Their paths crossed again while they were acting in the theatre. Their first break came during the summer of 1938 when Judy Tuvim, later Judy Holliday, saw Green perform and was impressed with his energy and humor. Holliday met Max Gordon, the proprietor of the Village Vanguard, and asked him to consider hiring a group that did songs and skits.

Holliday asked Green if they could get a group together, and, when Green saw Comden at an audition, he asked her if she would be interested. They both knew an actor who was looking for a job, and five of them, including Judy Holliday, formed a group called "The Revuers."

## Highlights of Their Early Work

Initially, each member of the group earned $5.00 for one show a week. They couldn't afford to pay royalties for outside material, so they wrote their own—skits, music, and lyrics. The five performers met to "brainstorm," and Betty recorded the ideas that were generated. When they identified a good idea, they improvised on it. It was a cooperative effort, and no one kept a record of who contributed what. Their shows were humorous, satirical skits about the social mores of the 1930s. Eventually, they did two shows, five nights a week. A favorable review by Dick Manson of the New York *Post* increased their audience significantly.

In November 1939, The Revuers performed at the Rainbow Room on the top floor of Rockefeller Plaza. They did their well-developed impersonations of Noel Coward, Joan Crawford, Queen Victoria, and Oscar Wilde, as well as sketches of Broadway, Hollywood, and the New York World's Fair. Patrons at the Rainbow Room were conservative, and what worked at the Village Vanguard didn't work there. They received respectable reviews, but they thought that they had "bombed."

In October 1940, The Revuers performed five times a day for three weeks at Radio City Music Hall. In December, they returned to the Village Vanguard. They were disappointed, because it seemed that they were back where they started. The following year they toured the country as far west as St. Louis.

In 1942, Irving Caesar, the lyricist who wrote "Swanee" and "Tea for Two" cast The Revuers in a musical called *My Dear Public*. The play had a short run in New York, so The Revuers returned to the nightclub circuit. They had a long engagement at the Blue Angel, Max Gordon's cabaret on the east side of Manhattan, and then went on a road tour, which included an engagement at the Blackstone Hotel in Chicago.

On January 4, 1942, Betty Comden married Siegfried Schutzman, who subsequently changed his name to Steven Kyle. He was an artist about to enter the U.S. Army. Later, they had two children; Susanna was born in 1949, and Alan was born in 1953. Their friend Leonard Bernstein wrote "Anniversary for Susanna Kyle" to celebrate the birth of their first child.

During the summer of 1942, The Revuers went to Los Angeles, where Hollywood agent Kurt Frings obtained roles for them in the film version of the popular radio show, *Duffy's Tavern*. However, upon their arrival in Hollywood, they were told that the film had been cancelled. The Revuers obtained an engagement at the Trocadero night club; they opened to rave reviews. Agents offered Judy Holliday movie contracts, but none of the other members of The Revuers received any offers. Holliday didn't want to accept a contract with Twentieth Century-Fox unless the other members of The Revuers were included. Comden and Green told her that she would be foolish not to take the studio's offer.

On completion of their engagement at the Trocadero, Comden returned to New York where her husband was on leave from the Army. She planned to returned to Hollywood when Kyle's furlough was over, but Adolph called her to tell her that he was coming to New York to visit his mother who was ill. Temporarily, they were unemployed.

Comden and Green, without the rest of The Revuers, returned to perform at Max Gordon's Blue Angel in Manhattan. From this point onward in their careers, they continued to perform but became more creators than performers. In between performances at the Blue Angel, they were visited by Leonard Bernstein, Paul Feigay, and Oliver Smith. The three men were motivated by the success of the ballet, *Fancy Free,* which Bernstein and Jerome Robbins had presented with the Ballet Theatre.

Oliver Smith, who had designed the set for the ballet, and Paul Feigay wanted to produce a musical about three sailors on leave in New York; the ballet version had premiered at the Metropolitan Opera House on April 18, 1944, to rave reviews. They asked Betty and Adolph to write the script and the lyrics for the musical. During the summer that year, Comden and Green wrote the libretto and the lyrics while Bernstein wrote the music.

Betty and Adolph wrote lively parts for themselves into the script of *On the Town*. They had to audition, but they were chosen for the parts. Adolph was one of the three sailors, Ozzie, and Betty played Claire de Loone, an anthropologist. Claire is fascinated by Ozzie because, in her opinion, his appearance is that of a prehistoric man. The storyline is about three sailors pursuing "Miss Turnstiles," whose picture they had seen on a poster in a subway train. The success of the musical was virtually assured when George Abbot agreed to direct the play. He was the only one of the creators of the musical who was over thirty years old.

The team that created *On the Town,* except Bernstein who wasn't available, immediately started work on another musical. Morton Gould wrote the music for *Billion Dollar Baby,* which opened at the Alvin Theatre on December 21, 1945. The musical, which starred Joan McCracken, was about the roaring twenties. It was only moderately successful, but Comden and Green now had two successful plays to their credit. They wanted to return to Hollywood to work on a film.

Metro-Goldwyn-Mayer gave them an offer to write a screenplay based on the Broadway musical about college life, *Good News,* working with the producer, Arthur Freed. Initially, Comden and Green weren't enthusiastic about the project, which was a revision of a 1930 film. They wrote a new screenplay that incorporated most of the songs from the original script. However, they added to the original lyrics and wrote a catchy song, "The French Lesson," about the subject that the football hero was flunking. June Allyson, Peter Lawford, and Joan McCracken starred in the film. *Good News* was considered to be the best college-theme musical produced in the 1940s.

Comden's and Green's second screenplay was *The Barkleys of Broadway,* starring Fred Astaire and Ginger Rogers. It was about a married couple, an acting and dancing team, who danced well together but whose off-stage relationship was stormy. It was one of the top-rated films of 1949, and it received a nomination for a Screenwriters Guild Award.

Comden's and Green's next Hollywood project was to write the lyrics for four songs for *Take Me Out to the Ball*

*Game,* starring Gene Kelly and Frank Sinatra. The story was written by Gene Kelly and his assistant and friend, Stanley Donen. Gene Kelly was one of the few people in Hollywood that Betty and Adolph knew when they moved west. They had met Kelly in 1939 when they had performed at the Westport Country Playhouse. *Take Me Out to the Ball Game,* which was released in 1949, was another successful movie.

Comden's and Green's greatest success in 1949 was the movie made from their Broadway musical, *On The Town,* which was co-directed by Gene Kelly and Stanley Donen. The producer, Arthur Freed, considered Bernstein's music to be too avant-garde, so he asked Roger Edens to write the music and Betty and Adolph to write the lyrics for eight new songs.

Only four songs of Bernstein's original Broadway score were used in the film. The three sailors on the town were played by Gene Kelly, Frank Sinatra, and Jules Munshin, the same trio from *Take Me Out to the Ball Game. On The Town,* which premiered at Radio City Music Hall on December 30, 1949, earned Comden and Green a Screenwriters Guild Award.

## Leonard Bernstein — Friend and Collaborator

In the summer of 1937, Adolph played the Pirate King in the *Pirates of Penzance* at Camp Onata, a boys' summer camp near Pittsfield, Massachusetts. The music counselor that summer was a young Harvard music student, Leonard Bernstein. Bernstein sat down at the piano and played a practical joke on

Green. He mentioned that he was going to play a Shostakovich prelude. Green asked, "Which one?" Bernstein responded, "This one," but instead he played a series of dissonances. Green told him that it wasn't any of Shostakovich's preludes. Bernstein laughed; he had played the trick many times before, and the listeners always had claimed to recognize the music.

They both possessed a knowledge of music and a sense of humor, and they became close friends. Bernstein's younger brother, Burton, wrote that Green was "capable of performing—a capella and with every orchestral instrument outrageously imitated—just about any symphonic work, classical or modern, down to the last cymbal crash."

In June 1939, Leonard Bernstein graduated from Harvard University and moved to New York to look for a job. He shared an apartment in Greenwich Village with Green and occasionally filled in as the pianist for The Revuers. Frequently, Bernstein played the piano at the parties that he and Green attended. At one of these parties, Betty Comden met Bernstein. She went home, awakened her mother from a sound sleep, and told her, "I met a real genius tonight."

Bernstein discussed his future with Dimitri Mitropoulos, who told him that he had all the necessary skills to be a conductor. Bernstein applied to the Julliard School in September and was told that no more applications were being accepted. He enrolled at the Curtis Institute in Philadelphia and was on his way to becoming famous.

In 1942, The Revuers were cast in a musical called *My*

*Dear Public,* which played in Philadelphia before opening in New York. Leonard Bernstein had completed his conductor training at the Curtis Institute but was unable to find a steady job so he hung out with the cast of *My Dear Public.* Bernstein impressed Irving Ceasar, who had done the casting for the play. He compared the young man to George Gershwin. Ceasar found Bernstein a job in New York making piano arrangements for a music publishing company.

The following year, Artur Rodzinski was appointed conductor of the New York Philharmonic and appointed Bernstein his assistant. On November 14, 1943, Bruno Walter, the guest conductor, was ill, and Maestro Rodzinski was snowed in at his Stockbridge farm. Twenty-five-year-old Bernstein conducted the New York Philharmonic that evening and made the most of the opportunity. The performance was broadcast nationally on radio, and Bernstein woke up the next morning a famous man. However, he and Comden and Green continued to collaborate on musicals.

In June 1944, Bernstein entered the hospital to have an operation for a deviated septum to relieve his chronic sinus problems. At the same time, Adolph had his enlarged tonsils removed. They were operated on the same day by the same doctor and shared a hospital room, so that they could continue to work on the musical, *On the Town.* As they recuperated, Betty worked with them in their room. When friends visited they became a bit rowdy, which irritated the hospital staff. One nurse upset by Bernstein's antics commented, "He may be God's gift to music, but I'd hate to tell you where he gives me a pain."

In August, Bernstein accompanied the Ballet Theatre to California to conduct *Fancy Free*. He composed the music for *On the Town* en route and while he was in California. He wrote the first major number, "New York, New York," as the train sped across the flat farmland of Nebraska. *On the Town* was completed that autumn and opened at the Adelphi Theatre on December 28, 1944. Critics praised the book by the young writing team, Comden and Green, and called the work "fresh." In particular, they liked the integration of the storyline with the choreography and the songs. Comden and Green maintained their friendship and collaboration with Leonard Bernstein over the years.

### *Singin' in the Rain*—A Project That Didn't Go Smoothly

In 1951, Comden and Green received an urgent call from Metro-Goldwyn-Mayer to return to Hollywood to write an original story, screenplay, and lyrics for a new musical film. The screenplay was about the transition from silent movies to the talkies. The lead character, who began his career in vaudeville, was to be shown making the successful transition from silent films.

They were to work for producer Arthur Freed in the Thalberg Administration Building. At their first meeting with Freed, they were told that they had been assigned to write the story and screenplay, but that the songs used would be ones already written by lyricist Arthur Freed (the producer) and composer Nacio Herb Brown. The movie was to be called

*Singin' in the Rain.*

Comden and Green erupted. They had been told that they were to write the lyrics, and, furthermore, their previous agent had told them that their contract stated that they were to create the lyrics unless the music was written by Irving Berlin, Cole Porter, or Richard Rodgers and Oscar Hammerstein. They stomped off the job and threatened to return to New York. They accused Freed of breaking his promises; the strained relations continued for two weeks.

Finally, their new agent, Irving Lazar, suggested that they read their contract. The clause about Berlin, Porter, and Rodgers and Hammerstein wasn't there. Lazar told them "anyone can write lyrics for your picture: Berlin, Porter, Rodgers and Hammerstein, Freed, Karloff, Lugosi, Johnny Weissmuller—you name it. My suggestion is you write 'Singin' in the Rain' at the top of a page, followed by 'Fade-in,' and don't stop until you come to 'That's All, Folks.'"

Roger Edens, the associate producer and music director, played the songs as the collaborators searched for a storyline. Initially, they had difficulty coming up with a usable plot. For example, the song, "The Wedding of the Painted Doll," might have suggested a story about a painted doll that got married. Many of the songs are now well-known, including "Broadway Melody," "Fit as a Fiddle," "You Were Meant for Me," and the title song, "Singin' in the Rain." The only song in the movie for which Comden and Green wrote the lyrics was "Moses Supposes His Toes-es Are Roses."

They also had difficulty deciding on the time period in

which the movie should be set. Many of these songs had been written between 1929 and 1931 for the first musical movies made. This was during the time of transition between silent film and the "talkies." Instead of placing the story in contemporary times or picking a period like the gay nineties, they decided to use the time during which the songs were written.

Knowing who would play the lead was important, because that would affect the storyline. Initially, Howard Keel was considered for the role. Freed wanted Gene Kelly for the starring role, but Kelly was busy filming *An American in Paris*. Because of the delays in getting started on the story and screenplay, Gene Kelly became available, since he had finished making *An American in Paris*. Kelly was so enthusiastic about the plans for *Singin' in the Rain* that he agreed to co-direct the film with Stanley Donen.

After the first month of planning the screenplay, Comden and Green had three possible openings:

- the premiére of an important silent movie in New York
- an action sequence from the silent move being premiéred in New York, with the star meeting a girl in New York, losing her, and returning to Hollywood
- an interview for a magazine, with the star in Hollywood relating a fantasized life story.

Comden and Green couldn't decide which opening to use. The work just wasn't moving along smoothly; they were depressed. They seriously considered returning the money that MGM had given them, packing up, and returning to Manhattan.

About that time, Betty's husband, Steve Kyle, arrived from New York. He wasn't surprised to see them slumped over in near despair. He had seen them this way before on earlier projects that weren't going well. Steve wasn't a writer; he was an artist with a successful merchandising business. However, they frequently used him as a sounding board, and he had been a valuable source of ideas. He laughed when he read the material. They asked him which opening they should use; he suggested that they use all three openings.

Steve's suggestion resulted in an epiphany of realization that all of the action could take place on Hollywood Boulevard instead of on Fifth Avenue in New York. The change wasn't significant; however, Comden observed:

> It seems pitifully obvious now, bordering on the moronic, but at the time we felt like [Jean Francois] Champollion deciphering the Rosetta Stone. From here on, the gates were open and the writing of the screenplay gushed in a relatively exuberant flow. We tapped the roots of our memories and experiences without editing ourselves when our ideas got wild, satirical, and extravagantly nonsensical. To our gratified surprise, not only did Roger seem delighted with it all, but Arthur, to whom we read each section as we completed it, gave his happy approval.[14]

The final approval was given by Dore Schary, who had recently replaced L. B. Mayer as head of MGM.

Meetings began with Gene Kelly and Stanley Donen in

which they applied their skills in integrating the various elements of the musical. Comden and Green realized that the success of the film was to a large extent due to what they referred to as the "four-way mental radar" among them. Kelly and Donen were professionals who excelled at the execution of the performance while sustaining a light, carefree air.

They all knew from their first reading that the musical involved a scene that took place in the rain. What none of them realized was that "here Gene Kelly performs the most notable solo musical number of his career," or, in other words, "miracle happens here." Fortunately, the song, "The Wedding of the Painted Doll," was replaced with "Make 'Em Laugh," in which Donald O'Connor pulled out all the stops and did a classic, upbeat vaudeville / clown number.

Comden and Green returned to New York after completing the screenplay for *Singin' in the Rain* to write sketches and lyrics for *Two on the Aisle*. They were in Philadelphia, helping to whip that revue into shape prior to playing on Broadway, when they received an urgent call from Kelly and Donen. They were asked to drop everything and write a romantic scene in an empty sound stage where Kelly would sing one song and do one dance with Debbie Reynolds. This was to replace a lengthy love scene in which Kelly and Reynolds danced and did a medley of songs involving multiple sets.

Comden and Green unplugged themselves from a frantic effort to finish *Two on the Aisle* and projected themselves back to the atmosphere of *Singin' in the Rain*. Their efforts clicked, and the movie was wildly successful. It is consistent- ly rated as one of the ten best musical films; in one rating, it is considered to be third best. Critic Pauline Kael wrote: "This exuberant and malicious satire of Hollywood in the late twen- ties is perhaps the most enjoyable of all movie musicals—just about the best Hollywood musical of all time."

Comden and Green won their second Screenwriters Guild Award for the movie, which opened at Radio City Music hall on March 27, 1952. The film in which the writers of the screenplay almost gave up and went home—not once, but twice—turned out to be one of the best ever. Comden and Green have provided us with an example of the value of per- severance. Few significant accomplishments proceed steadily without problems from beginning to end.

## Highlights of Their Later Work

After finally completing work on *Singin' in the Rain,* Comden and Green returned to New York to finish revising the skits and the lyrics for the revue, *Two on the Aisle,* which starred Bert Lahr and Delores Gray. Lahr, who was a talented come- dian, is remembered mainly for his role as the Cowardly Lion in *The Wizard of Oz.* Delores Gray, an accomplished singer and comedienne, had her first success starring in the role of Annie Oakley in *Annie Get Your Gun* in London. *Two on the Aisle* was the first of many musicals in which Comden and Green collaborated with composer Jule Styne.

Their next screenplay was *The Band Wagon,* which starred Fred Astaire and was directed by Vincent Minnelli.

The movie was based on the 1931 Broadway revue starring Fred Astaire and his sister, Adele. It was about a film star whose career was fading being invited to New York by friends, a married writing team much like Comden and Green, to star in a Broadway musical. The film, which received an Academy Award nomination, debuted at Radio City Music Hall in July 1953.

Comden's and Green's next musical, *Wonderful Town,* opened at the Winter Garden Theatre on February 25, 1953, to rave reviews. It was based on the 1940 play, *My Sister Eileen,* which, in turn, was based on Ruth McKenney's stories about herself and her lively sister in New York in the 1930s. Rosalind Russell starred as Ruth, as she had in the 1940 movie version.

Betty and Adolph were pleased to be working again with their friend, Leonard Bernstein, who wrote the music for the play. George Abbott directed the musical, which won a Tony Award for Outstanding Musical of the Year. Rosalind Russell won the award as Outstanding Musical Actress and Comden and Green won a Donaldson Award for *Wonderful Town,* which played for 559 performances.

In May 1956, Betty and Adolph reviewed the first draft of *Bells Are Ringing* with Judy Holliday to see if they could entice her to star in the play. The story was about a switch-board operator at an answering service who takes a personal interest in the service's customers. The music was written by Jule Styne, and the musical was directed by Jerome Robbins. It opened at the Shubert Theatre on November 29, 1956, and ran for 924 performances. Judy Holliday won a 1957 Tony Award for her role.

Phyllis Newman met Adolph Green when she was Judy Holliday's understudy in *Bells Are Ringing.* Adolph visited the theatre frequently because he was a friend of both Judy Holliday and the leading man, Sydney Chaplin, the son of Charlie Chaplin. Phyllis was attracted to Adolph, but she was intimidated by "his age, his reputation as an intellectual, his success, and, most of all, by his mind-boggling eccentricity." In her book, *Just in Time,* Phyllis comments about Adolph: "He always looks suspicious and guilty, as though he has just done something he shouldn't have. He rarely looks you straight in the eye. He seems to be hiding something, but I have never found out what it is."

Adolph and Phyllis dated, and she was intimidated again—this time by his famous friends, such as Lauren Bacall and Leonard Bernstein. She realized that she was in love with Adolph after seeing him and Betty perform in *A Party With Betty Comden and Adolph Green* at the Westport Playhouse in Connecticut. Phyllis and Adolph were married on January 31, 1960.

Work on the film version of *Bells Are Ringing* began on October 6, 1959. Judy Holliday reprised her role as the switchboard operator; Vincent Minnelli directed. The movie opened at Radio City Music Hall on June 23, 1960. Betty and Adolph won their third Screenwriters Guild Award for the screenplay.

Also that year, Comden and Green wrote the lyrics for *Do*

*Re Mi,* a musical based on the novella by Garson Kanin. Jule Styne wrote the music. Phil Silvers starred as Hubie Cram, a nobody with aspirations of fame and fortune. Comedienne Nancy Walker contributed a memorable performance as Mrs. Cram. The play opened on December 26, 1960, at the St. James Theatre and ran for over 400 performances. The song, "Make Someone Happy" by Comden, Green, and Styne, was the hit song from the musical.

Betty's and Adolph's hit of the 1970s was *Applause,* which opened at the Palace Theatre on March 30, 1970 with Lauren Bacall in the leading role. They wrote the book; the music was by Charles Strouse and the lyrics were by Lee Adams. When Bacall was asked by the producers about Comden and Green doing the book she hesitated because they were good friends, and she didn't want to mix friendship and career. She agreed because "they were so smart and funny, and talented."

*Applause* was based on the film *All About Eve,* which starred Anne Baxter and Bette Davis. The musical won the Tony Award for Best Musical in 1970, and Bacall won the Award for Best Actress in a Musical. Comden, Green, Adams, and Strouse all won Tony Awards that year. *Applause* ran for 840 performances on Broadway.

On March 17, 1980, Betty and Adolph were voted into the Songwriters Hall of Fame. In 1981, they were selected by drama critics and editors for entrance into the Theatre Hall of Fame. Requirements for membership are a Broadway career of at least twenty-five years and more than five major credits.

They continued to write plays and lyrics into the 1990s, in addition to teaching at New York University's Tisch School of the Arts.

On May 29, 1991, Betty and Adolph were presented with the Johnny Mercer Award for Lifetime Achievement by the Songwriters Hall of Fame. On December 8, 1991, the collaborators were presented the Kennedy Center Honors for Lifetime Achievement in the Performing Arts, a fine capstone for their careers.

Gracie Allen and George Burns
Courtesy University of Southern California
Cinema-Television Library

**Chapter 3**

## GRACIE ALLEN AND GEORGE BURNS

*"Gracie was my partner in our act, my best friend, my wife and my lover, and the mother of our two children. We were a team, both on and off the stage. Our relationship was simple, I fed her the straight lines, and she fed me. She made me famous as the only man in America who could get a laugh by complaining, 'My wife understands me.'"*[15]

*George Burns in Gracie, A Love Story*

Gracie Allen and George Burns were together as a team for almost forty years in a business known for short-term partnerships and even shorter-term marriages. They performed together in vaudeville, radio, and television until a few years prior to Gracie's death. Gracie played the role of the dizzy dame in their performances; in life, she was anything but her show-business image.

George readily admitted that Gracie was much more than half of their act, and that he was merely the straight man. He handled their business arrangements, and he wrote much of their material; however, he acknowledged that the audiences came to see and hear Gracie, not him. Timing was one of George's strengths in their work together. Gracie had most of the dialogue and never muffed a line; she was a professional in every sense of the word.

George Burns and Gracie Allen began in vaudeville in 1922, became a long-running act with top billing on the Keith-Orpheum Theatres circuit, and made fourteen one-reel motion pictures. They had supporting roles in twelve feature films, including "The Big Broadcast" series of 1932, 1936, and 1937, "International House" in 1933 with W. C. Fields, "Many Happy Returns" in 1934, "A Damsel in Distress" in 1937 with Fred Astaire, and "College Swing" in 1938. They also had a network radio show for eighteen years, and, from 1950 to 1958, they starred in "The George Burns and Gracie Allen Show" on television; both programs highlighted Gracie's "illogical logic."

**Working Together**

George realized Gracie's importance to their act from the beginning. He openly acknowledged that Gracie carried the show. She had considerably more memorization of lines to do because she had over two-thirds of the dialogue. Her role required that she say her lines correctly to get laughs. George observed:

> ... there was a lot more to Gracie than that funny little girl whose mind was made up— mostly by me and our writers. Gracie was a beautiful, elegant lady with real style and class. You never saw Gracie looking anything but perfect. And she was charming. And she was very smart, smart enough to become the dumbest woman in show-business history. Gracie was a great actress. I don't think she ever received enough credit for that. She was nothing like the dizzy character she played....[16]
>
> There never was any professional jealousy between me and Gracie. Acts would run into trouble when they began competing for laughs. We never did; Gracie got the laughs, and at the end of the night, I got to bring Gracie home. It was so obvious that she was the whole act that we made it part of the act.[17]

On one occasion, George identified the ingredients of a successful marriage. "Obviously, sex is important. Being able to talk to each other openly and honestly is vital. A sense of humor is a necessity. You've got to be able to share. But if a man really wants his marriage to work, the one thing he has to remember is: Never play cards with your wife ... That's it, that's the secret. You can solve every other problem. But a married couple that plays cards together is just a fight that hasn't started yet."

Division of labor was a key to the success of George's and Gracie's marriage. George thought that one reason they had a good marriage was their different responsibilities. In one of his less serious moments, George observed: "I made all the decisions concerning our career and finances, while Gracie's job was to run the house, raise the children, and make sure that we always had enough dresses, hats, and furs."

Although Gracie's scripts were written for her, if she didn't like a line she refused to say it that way. The line was either rewritten or omitted. On rare occasions, she rejected an entire script. Although she was a born actress, she worked hard in preparing for a performance. George commented that she "could dissect a performance as well as anyone I've ever known."

George described the importance of Gracie's role to their television show.

> Most of my work is behind the scenes. When we work, particularly now that we are in television, the main burden of the performance is on Gracie. If you look at the show, you will notice that she is on with an enormous amount of unnatural dialogue almost the entire time. As she is a complete perfectionist, she is always letter perfect, which means days of memorizing before we shoot. She just gets one

show committed to memory, shoots it; and
then before she has a chance to take a deep
breath, next week's script has arrived and she
starts on that.

On the set she gives absolutely no trouble and
makes no demands. She arrives on time, does
the job, jokes with the crew, and generally
behaves less like a star that any actress I ever
knew ... [18]

Occasionally, George had to trick Gracie into doing something that she didn't want to do. For example, they were asked to be in a picture with Fred Astaire and to dance with him in one scene. George knew that Gracie could dance well enough to do it, but he wasn't sure that he would be able to keep up with Astaire. However, lack of talent had never stopped him before, so he just had to convince Gracie that she was up to it. He talked her into at least trying.

George remembered a whisk-broom dance from vaudeville. He located one of the two partners that had performed the dance, paid him for the rights to it, and asked him to teach it to him and to Gracie. They used the dance for their audition with Fred, who said, "It's great! It goes in the picture just the way it is." George had located a dance that Fred hadn't seen, and, instead of being nervous dancing for him, taught him the dance.

George summarized his relationship with Gracie:

My belief is that a lot of show-business marriages go on the rocks because the man and the woman are in competition rather than in partnership. With us, it's very simple: Gracie takes the lead on stage; I take it, off. We both have our own departments. She stays in hers, and I'm into everybody's. Gracie's had always been the greater acting talent; she is the star, but you'd never know it. She has always allowed me to advise her, direct her, and to speak for us. One thing I don't do for her. She thinks for herself, and when she's made up her mind, that's it....[19]

George Burns and Gracie Allen performed together for thirty-six years and were happily married for thirty-eight years. Although Gracie performed by herself in a few radio shows and movies, she and George never performed with other partners until George performed with Carol Channing after Gracie retired. Their successful marriage was never interrupted by a separation. They knew each other's strengths, and each let the other person do the things that he or she excelled at doing.

Above all, they never competed with each other. Gracie may have been portrayed as a "dumb Dora" and George may have been "only a straight man," but together they showed us how a man and woman can perform as a team—both in their professional lives and in their personal lives.

### George Burns—Training for the Stage

Nathan Birnbaum (George Burns), the ninth of twelve children, was born on January 20, 1896, on Pitt Street in New York City. The family was poor, and Nathan and a neighbor picked up lumps of coal from the street and brought them home to heat the apartment. Their friends would see their pockets bulging with coal and call out, "Here come the Burns Brothers," after the Burns Coal Company that served the neighborhood. Burns became George's stage name.

George's first experience performing was with the Pee-Wee Quartet at the age of seven. The quartet sang in saloons and on the Staten Island Ferry. George said that the passengers on the ferry had a choice of listening to them or of jumping overboard; their quartet had the classic captive audience. When George was thirteen, he and a friend opened B-B's College of Dancing. Later in life, Burns recalled that, "We got most of our clients right off the immigration boats at Ellis Island. We told them one of the first requirements of becoming a United States citizen was a $5 course of dancing lessons. Dishonest, you say? Maybe. But have you ever been hungry?"

Burns began a series of vaudeville acts, which included a seal act and performing as a trick roller skater. The acts were so poor that he had to change his name frequently to improve his chances of being hired at the next theatre. He was known as Jimmy Delight, Billy Pierce, Maurice Valente, Jack Garfield, and Jed Jackson. At various times, he was either Brown or Williams of Brown and Williams. He was even known as Buddy Links in an act called Burns and Links. Burns' last partner before meeting Gracie Allen was Billy Lorraine, who stuttered off stage but not, thankfully, on stage.

Rena Arnold and Company was on the bill with Burns and Lorraine at the Union Hill Theatre in New Jersey. Gracie was performing with Rena Arnold and heard that Burns and Lorraine were splitting up. She asked George if he wanted a new partner. Initially, Gracie was the "straight man" and George had the funny lines until George realized that the audience was laughing at Gracie. They reversed roles, and George became the straight man.

## Gracie Allen—Preparation for Vaudeville

Gracie Ethel Cecile Rosalie Allen was born in San Francisco on July 26, 1906. She had her own dancing act at the age of four. After graduating from the Star of the Sea School in San Francisco, she joined her sisters in an act called The Four Colleens. One of her sisters left the show and Gracie and the other two joined Larry Reilly and Company in a dramatic act. When one of her sisters in the act returned to San Francisco and the other one married, Gracie became the "and Company."

One night Gracie went to the theatre in Hoboken on opening night and saw that the name of their act had been changed to "Larry Reilly." She didn't mind that the act wasn't called Reilly and Allen, "but no billing I couldn't stand." She left the act. She was eighteen and living alone in New York City. Her sisters sent her money for living expenses. She shared an apartment with two friends, Mary Kelly and Rena Arnold. After six months without working, she enrolled in secretarial school.

Gracie met Benny Ryan, a successful actor and songwriter. They dated, and he wrote an act for her. After Rena

Arnold introduced Gracie to George, they met at a restaurant in mid-town Manhattan to work out the details of their act together. The act that Benny Ryan had written for Gracie required a $300 set, and George's act didn't use a set. Since neither of them had $300, they did George's act.

Gracie's roommate, Mary Kelly, dated Jack Benny. Jack and George became good friends; George's ability to put Jack into uncontrollable laughter began about this time. However, Jack had a problem. He was in love with Mary Kelly, a Catholic who was determined to marry a Catholic.

**The Burns and Allen Vaudeville Act**

From the beginning of their act together, Gracie played the role of "dumb Dora." She played the role with a serious face, as though she was right and the rest of the world was wrong. She was enough of a natural comedienne to pull it off even when their material was weak. One of the lines that gained recognition for them was George's comment in disbelief, "You're dizzy," to one of her lines. She responded, "Well, I'm glad I'm dizzy because boys like dizzy girls and I like boys." George replied, "Well, I'm glad you're glad you're dizzy," "And I'm glad that you're glad that I'm glad I'm dizzy." "And I'm glad ... " They could pull it off, but you had to be there in person to appreciate it.

After working with Gracie for awhile, George fell in love with her. His love developed over a period of time. George observed, "There wasn't a moment when I looked at Gracie and suddenly realized I was in love. It just happened. Love is a lot like a backache, it doesn't show up on X-rays, but you know it's there." George proposed to Gracie many times, but she intended to marry Benny Ryan.

George's and Gracie's relationship arrived at a critical stage at a Christmas party in Gracie's apartment with their friends. Benny Ryan was out of town. George gave Gracie a silver bracelet with a small diamond. She gave George a lounging robe with a card on which she had written, "To Nattie, with all my love." George read the card, laughed heartily, and said, "All your love? Ha, ha, ha. You don't even know what love means." Gracie began to cry and went into the bedroom and closed the door. George left the party alone.

Gracie had planned to call Benny Ryan to wish him a Merry Christmas, but she called George instead. She told him, "You can buy the wedding ring if you want to." George said, "You'll never be sorry." He didn't tell her that he had already spent $20 on a wedding ring. The next morning, he asked her why she changed her mind about marrying Benny Ryan. She explained, "You're the only boy who ever made me cry. And I decided that if you could make me cry, I must really love you." In January 1926, they were married in Cleveland while on a road trip.

Their vaudeville career had been a series of short engagements; however, six weeks after they were married, they signed a five-year contract with Keith-Orpheum. The apex for vaudeville performers was to perform at the Palace in New York. In 1928, as part of their contract with Keith-Orpheum, they performed at the Palace for the first time.

## Transition from Vaudeville to Radio and Television

In 1929, George and Gracie attended a party for Jack Benny given by his agent, Arthur Lyons. Lyons asked Benny whether he would like to earn $1,800 by making a nine-minute short film for Paramount the following morning. Benny wasn't able to do it, so George and Gracie made the film at the Astoria Studios in Queens the next day. This led to their doing four more short films at $3,500 each. Eventually, they made fourteen short films.

Their first full-length movie was "The Big Broadcast of 1932." By this stage of their careers, they had become radio stars. They first appeared on radio in England in 1929 to promote their stage shows. Their transition to radio was a smooth one; they simply dropped their dance routines. Eddie Cantor paved the way for vaudevillians moving to radio with his show for Chase and Sanborn. Sponsors began to look for other acts that could make the transition from vaudeville to radio.

Grape Nuts turned down Burns and Allen. A company executive said, "Gracie will never make it on radio. Her voice is too high." They appeared, successfully, with Rudy Vallee on his Fleischmann's Yeast Hour and with Guy Lombardo on his radio show for General Cigar. When Lombardo left to do another show, General Cigar signed George and Gracie to do "The Adventures of Gracie." Their theme song "Love Nest" from vaudeville was used for the radio show.

A gimmick that brought Burns and Allen to the public's attention was the hunt for Gracie's "missing brother." Gracie really did have a brother, but he wasn't missing. They appeared on Jack Benny's show and Rudy Vallee's show with the search for the "lost brother." This gimmick caused Gracie's real brother considerable grief from journalists, photographers, and the public. Finally, he disappeared, and Gracie's brother really was missing. However, the ruse succeeded in putting Burns and Allen in the national spotlight.

In 1950, "The George Burns and Gracie Allen Show" moved from radio to television, retaining the "Love Nest" theme song and the members of the cast. Bea Benaderet played the Burns' neighbor, Blanche, and Hal March was Blanche's husband, Harry. George occasionally stepped out of the plot and spoke directly to the audience. George claimed that technique as his innovation. He admitted, however, that he might owe something to Thorton Wilder's "Our Town." The show always concluded with George's line: "Say good night, Gracie." Gracie always obliged by saying, "Good night, Gracie."

## Gracie's Campaign for President as a Candidate of the Surprise Party

Public interest in the Burns and Allen radio show was increased by Gracie's presidential campaign in 1940. Franklin Roosevelt was the Democratic Party's candidate, Wendell Wilkie ran on the Republican ticket, and Gracie Allen was the presidential candidate of the Surprise Party. Initially, her campaign was scheduled to run for two weeks. However, public interest motivated her sponsors to lengthen her campaign.

Gracie said that she had an excellent chance of winning because "half of all the married people in this country are women."

Gracie's campaign gained momentum when the Union Pacific Railroad decided to participate and the city of Omaha, Nebraska, offered to host her nominating convention. In 1939, the railroad and the city had sponsored an Old West celebration called Golden Spike Days to promote the movie "Union Pacific." The activity attracted so many tourists that the city wanted to repeat it. The Union Pacific Railroad offered to provide Gracie with a campaign train for her whistlestop tour from Los Angeles to Omaha. Upon her arrival in Omaha, she would dedicate their new coliseum.

It was a great publicity stunt, but Gracie didn't want to do it. She disliked making speeches, and she didn't think that she could pull it off. Only when her sister Hazel and Mary Kelly offered to come along with the entire writing staff of their radio show did Gracie give in and agree to do it. Gracie's campaign slogan, "It's in the bag" was accompanied by an illustration of a kangaroo holding a baby in her pouch.

Over 250,000 people greeted her train, including 15,000 on her arrival in Omaha. On May 17, 8,000 cheering delegates nominated Gracie for the office of President of the United States. She lost the election, but she received hundreds of write-in votes and the city of Memoninee, Michigan, nominated her for mayor. After the campaign, George and Gracie returned to the routine of doing their weekly radio show.

## George's Ability to Make Jack Benny Pound the Floor

George and Gracie had many friends in Hollywood; however, Jack Benny and Mary Livingstone were their closest friends. George had the ability to get Jack to laugh so hard that he would get down and pound the floor. An example of this occurred one evening when the two couples had an expensive dinner at Dave Chasen's Restaurant:

> Jack decided, "Let's get Dave Chasen to pick up the check tonight." George asked, "How do we do that, Jack?" Jack replied, "We're probably his best customers, so after dinner I'll call him over and tell him, 'Dave, if George Burns pays this check I'm never coming in here again.' then you say, 'And if Jack pays this check, I won't come in here again.' You know Dave, he'll say, 'Fellas—stop fighting,' and he'll pick it up."
>
> After dinner, Jack called Dave Chasen over to our table. "Dave," he said, "if George Burns gets this check, I'm not coming in here again." Then Jack looked at me. I smiled at him and took a long puff on my cigar. I looked at Dave Chasen and smiled. Never said a word. Jack pounded the floor so hard he almost dropped the check.[20]

The most outrageous example of George's humor occurred at a party at Jack's home. About 150 people were invited, and as far as George could tell, everyone was having a good time. As related by George:

Jack took me aside and said, "I don't think the party's moving." George observed, "Sure it's moving. Everybody's talking and drinking." Jack said, "I'm in show business too, you know. I know if a party's moving. This one isn't ..." "You want to liven it up a little," I said, "Here's what you do: go upstairs and take off your pants, put on one of Mary's big hats, then come downstairs in your shorts, wearing one of Mary's hats and playing your violin."

That appealed to him. "You think that'll make the party move?" "Oh yeah, sure." What else could I say? Trust me? Me? As soon as Jack went upstairs I got everybody's attention and said, "In a few minutes Jack is going to be coming downstairs in his shorts, wearing one of Mary's hats and playing the violin. When he does, don't pay any attention to him. Just ignore him completely."

A few minutes later Jack appeared at the top of the stairs, wearing his shorts and one of Mary's wide-brimmed hats, playing the violin. And everybody ignored him. It took him only a few minutes to realize that he was dressed in his underwear and a woman's hat, playing the violin and being ignored by one hundred and fifty people. And then he realized that I'd done it to him again. Jack pounded the floor. When he caught his breath, he looked at me and said, "Now, the party's moving."[21]

## Gracie's Retirement and Life After Gracie

Gracie developed heart disease, and her bouts of angina occurred more often. In 1958, she decided to retire. She told only her closest friends about her heart condition. Many people who didn't know about her health problem begged her not to retire. Also, many urged her to come out of retirement. She spent her time doing the things that she liked to do, such as playing cards and shopping.

After Gracie retired in 1958, George had his own show, "The George Burns Show," for a year and then teamed with Carol Channing on the nightclub circuit. In 1961, Gracie had a heart attack that slowed her down. She didn't go out as frequently at night, because she didn't have the energy.

In early 1964, her health began to fail. In August that year, she had another heart attack at home. She was taken to Cedars of Lebanon Hospital, where she died shortly after her arrival. George's devotion to Gracie was well-known. George arranged Episcopal rites for Gracie even though she was a Catholic. He explained: "I want to be buried with Gracie, and since I'm Jewish, I can't be buried in Catholic-consecrated ground. I hope the Episcopal rites were the right compromise." He frequently visited Gracie's grave at Forest Lawn Cemetery to "tell her everything I'm doing."

In 1976, George won an Oscar for best supporting actor in "The Sunshine Boys." He played God in "Oh, God!" in 1977 and in two sequels. He received a Grammy award for his recording of "Gracie," and wrote three popular books, *I Love Her, That's Why* in 1955, *Gracie: A Love Story* in 1988, and *All My Best Friends* in 1989.

In 1988, George received a John F. Kennedy Center for the Performing Arts Award for lifetime achievement. If Gracie had been alive, it would have been a joint award. George died on March 9, 1996, at the age of 100.

Lillian and Frank Gilbreth

# Chapter 4

## LILLIAN AND FRANK GILBRETH

*"Dad had enough gall to be divided into three parts [as ancient Gaul was], and the ability and poise to backstop the front he placed before the world.... One reason he had so many children—there were twelve of us—was that he was convinced anything he and Mother teamed up on was sure to be a success."*[22]

*Frank Gilbreth, Jr., and Ernestine Gilbreth Carey, in Cheaper by the Dozen*

Lillian and Frank Gilbreth, management consultants and specialists in motion study, were classic examples of two halves that make up the whole, or, more accurately, perfect the whole. He was not college educated; she had a Ph.D. in psychology. He began his working career as a bricklayer and moved into motion study from the trades. Before they married, he told her of his intention to teach her all facets of his construction business and of his consulting activities.

Although her undergraduate and masters degrees were in liberal arts, she didn't question his plan. She concentrated on the people side of their contracts and consulting work, thus compensating for one of his shortcomings.

Lillian and Frank Gilbreth, "efficiency experts," were an incredible team in scientific management, which became part of the field of industrial engineering. Frank's specialty was motion study, which he describes in the foreward of his 1911 book, *Motion Study, A Method for Increasing the Efficiency of the Workman:*

> The aim of motion study is to find and perpetuate the scheme of perfection. There are three stages in this study:
> 1. Discovering and classifying the best practice
> 2. Deducing the laws
> 3. Applying the laws to standardize practice, either for the purpose of increasing output or decreasing the hours of labor, or both. Standardizing the trades is the world's most important work today, and motion study is the first factor in that work.[23]

Lillian's strength was the application of psychology to scientific management in optimizing the human factors or the "people" component of their projects. Individually, each was missing part of the total package. Together, because they complemented each other extremely well, they were able to provide the complete package to their clients.

In the Introduction to Lillian's and Frank's 1917 book, *Applied Motion Study,* George Iles describes the authors:

> Frank B. Gilbreth is a versatile engineer, an untiring observer, an ingenious inventor, an economist to the tips of his fingers: first and chiefly he is a man.... Every page [of this book] has taken form with the aid and counsel of Mrs. Gilbreth, whose "Psychology of Management" is a golden gift to industrial philosophy. And thus, by viewing their facts from two distinct angles we learn how vital phases of industrial economy present themselves to a man and to a woman who are among the acutest investigators of our time.[24]

In the foreward of Edna Yost's book, *Frank and Lillian Gilbreth, Partners for Life,* A. A. Potter, Dean of Engineering at Purdue University summarized the personal characteristics of the Gilbreths:

> The outstanding characteristics of Frank Bunker Gilbreth were an alert and incisive mind; great ability to observe, analyze, synthesize, and correlate quickly and soundly; an insatiable intellectual curiosity and acquisitiveness; unbounded enthusiasm, zeal,

courage, and determination; marked optimism, great vitality, deep foresight, and a most remarkable manner of inspiring others to accept his ideas.

Lillian Moller Gilbreth, like her husband-partner, has an inate urge for the best and the first-rate, has unusual courage and optimism, loves people and work, has a talent for winning cooperation, and is a person of few antagonisms. Lillian Gilbreth not only won high recognition for her own contributions in motion study and applied psychology, but has preserved, enhanced, and increased the appreciation on the part of industry of the pioneering work of both Gilbreths in the field of management.[25]

Frank was ten years older than Lillian, and he died after they had been married twenty years. Lillian considered his love for her and his understanding of her needs to be more than that of couples who were married for over forty years.

## Frank's Early Life and Career

Frank Gilbreth was born on July 7, 1868, in Kendall's Mills, Maine, to Hiram Gilbreth and Martha Bunker Gilbreth. Hiram Gilbreth owned a successful hardware business and a 130-acre stock farm at which he developed racing horses, Jersey cows, and Chester and Yorkshire swine. Hiram was an excellent role model for his son, but he died before Frank entered first grade.

Martha was devastated by her husband's death; however,

she was financially secure. She sold the hardware business and the stock farm and moved to Andover, Massachusetts, where her three children could obtain a better education. Andover was the home of the Abbott Academy for girls and of Phillips Andover Academy for boys. She turned the management of her finances over to a brother-in-law in Boston.

One day the brother-in-law notified Martha that he had lost her money. Frank's sisters attended Abbott Academy, but Frank was too young to have entered Phillips Andover. Martha's father suggested that she move back home, but she decided to venture out on her own in Boston. Because she couldn't earn much income as an elementary school teacher, she rented a five-story house and opened a boardinghouse.

The boardinghouse prospered, and Frank's sisters earned good grades in the local schools. Frank, however, was only an average student. He wasn't challenged and didn't apply himself to his school subjects. On graduation from high school, Frank passed the entrance examinations to M.I.T., and he briefly considered enrolling there in electrical engineering.

Frank was confident, was willing to work hard, and wanted to earn money immediately—not in four years. Also, although his mother could afford to send him to college, he wasn't comfortable attending school while she supported him by running a boardinghouse. She was disappointed when he decided to learn the construction contracting business from the bottom up.

In July 1885, Frank joined the Thomas J. Whidden Company, contractors and builders, to learn the bricklaying trade. Shipbuilding was the only field that paid higher wages than the building trade. Because of its relatively high wages, construction attracted a higher grade of workmen than most of the other trades. Frank's first contacts were with these workers, and it influenced his attitude favorably toward his fellow workmen.

In his training for a supervisory job, he had the opportunity to learn other construction trades, such as carpentry, stone masonry, concrete work, roofing, tinsmithing, cast-iron work, and blacksmithing. However, bricklaying was his specialty. He was promoted to assistant foreman within two and a half years and then to foreman. His goal was to be a partner in the business within ten years. Thomas Whidden had given him the impression that the goal was achievable.

Frank had a favorable opinion of trade unions because of his positive experiences with them in the Boston area. The Massachusetts State Branch of the American Federation of Labor helped to stabilize the construction industry when the union was founded in 1887.

In 1892, Frank patented a scaffold for bricklayers that used platforms resting on adjustable frames at three levels. In a later design, it was suspended from jacks. His scaffold kept the rising wall at the same height for the bricklayer, thus minimizing stooping and stretching to lay the bricks. He submitted other patents, including one for the Gilbreth Waterproof Cellar, to prevent leaky cellars due to the daily rising of the tide in the Boston area.

At the age of twenty-seven, Frank decided that becoming

a partner of the Whidden Company in the short term was unlikely. Applications of his two inventions weren't receiving the attention that they required, so he left Whidden to establish his own business. He supported his mother and his Aunt Kit; however, he had no reservations about starting out on his own. His first employees were J. W. Buzzell, a civil engineering graduate of the Worcester Polytechnic Institute who became his second-in-command, and Anne Bowley, who efficiently ran his office.

Frank's third invention was a portable concrete mixer that relied on gravity to move concrete through a trough. This mixer was effective on small construction jobs and generated income to use on other projects. It also sold well in England.

Frank traveled widely, but he had time for meeting and dating young women. He was full of energy and had a quick sense of humor; he was a popular bachelor. His cousin, Minnie Bunker, arrived in Boston with three young women whom she was chaperoning on a trip to Europe. Lillian Moller was one of Minnie's charges. Frank met his future bride and partner while giving Minnie and the young women a sightseeing tour of Boston. Specifically, Frank and Lillian met on the second floor of the Boston Public Library in June 1903.

**Lillian's Early Life and Education**

Lillian Evelyn Moller, the second child of William Moller and Annie Delger Moller, was born in Oakland, California, on May 24, 1878. Annie was never in strong health after her firstborn child died in infancy. Lillie learned the responsibilities of caring for children and maintaining a home at an early age. Although she was born into a well-to-do family, her personality was shaped by the responsibility that was thrust upon her in her youth. Her next-oldest sister, Gertrude, and their cousin, Annie Florence, were considered to be prettier than she was. Lillie grew up thinking that she was unattractive to boys.

Lillie's childhood was a happy one in a family steeped in discipline of the children. She earned good grades in school. She observed, "I decided very young that since I couldn't be pretty I had to be smart." In high school, she studied music with the composer, John Metcalfe, and wrote poetry. She wanted to attend the University of California at Berkeley like her cousin, Annie Florence Brown, but her father initially disapproved because she would never have to support herself.

Finally, her father was willing to let her try Berkeley for a year. Lillie majored in modern languages and philosophy and also enrolled in history, mathematics, and science courses. She performed in student-produced plays in college, and she surprised herself with her confidence on the stage. She earned a Phi Beta Kappa key and was selected as the first woman Commencement Day speaker at the University.

Lillie enrolled in graduate school at Berkeley, wrote her master's thesis on Ben Jonson's "Bartholomew Fair," and planned to continue on with subjects leading to a Ph.D. degree. The summer that she received her M.A. degree was the one reserved for the planned trip to Europe with Minnie

Bunker, who taught at Oakland High School. The four women visited New York and Boston before boarding their ship bound for Europe.

### Frank and Lillian Meet and Marry

Frank gave the young women from California the grand tour of Boston in his new Winton-six motorcar. He included many new buildings on his tour and his conversation was sprinkled with observations such as "ready for occupancy forty-nine days after the contract was signed."

The Winton's engine quit on the trip, and Frank was confronted with a gathering of children taunting him about his shiny, new car that wouldn't run. Lillie was impressed with Frank's smiling, unruffled response to their teasing. Lillie kept the children's attention with stories while Frank obtained help in fixing the car. He was impressed with Lillie's ability to keep the children occupied.

Frank kidded Lillie until he realized that she didn't know how to take his teasing. He suggested that she use her literary background to help him write about his many experiences in the construction business. It was obvious to them that they were on the same wavelength. They knew that they would see each other again when Lillie returned from Europe.

1903 was an important year in both Frank's personal and business life. The fields of management and industrial engineering were not well defined at the time. Frederick W. Taylor presented his classic paper number 1003, "Shop Management," to the American Society of Mechanical

Engineers that year. Taylor's specialty was time study, but the field became known generically as scientific management.

Frank began compiling a book about his "Field System," in which he documented his thoughts on systematizing and standardizing organizations. His first draft was overly long, the pages weren't numbered, and it had no index until he sent it to Lillian in California to prepare it for publication.

His "Field System" included 299 numbered instructions and described Anne Bowley's filing system, the N file System. It was very clear on the manager / employee relationship; Frank described the disciplined boss who demanded obedience. In explaining his "Field System," Frank advocated the use of cost plus fixed fee contracts because they allowed construction to start earlier and move faster.

Although they were engaged for ten months, Frank and Lillian spent only about six days together between her return from Europe and their marriage in the Moller home in California on October 19, 1904. Frank met her ship upon her return from Europe and met her parents, who were impressed with him. He spent the Christmas holidays with Lillian and her family in Oakland. When he proposed to her, he made it clear that he expected her to participate in his business activities, and that his mother and his Aunt Kit would live with them after they were married.

Frank agreed with Lillian's continuing her work on a doctorate, but he suggested that she major rather than minor in psychology. He recognized the coming importance of the application of psychology in industry.

Lillian realized very early in their marriage that she had signed up for both a marital and a business partnership for life. Frank began to educate her immediately about his business. He started by saying "first I want to teach you about concrete and masonry. 'Bond' is the term we use to express the relationship of joints in masonry." Then he prepared a drawing so she that could understand the concept clearly.

Lillian had some adjustments to make. She was brought up in a sufficiently wealthy family that women were not expected to have a job. Frank had the reverse experience. His mother supported the family when his father died, and the wife of one of his fellow contractors ran her own contracting firm—sometimes competing for contracts with her husband.

Frank's mother, Martha, was in charge of the household, and Frank was frequently away on business trips. It was difficult for Lillian not to be mistress in her own house, but she had the personality to deal with it. In *Frank and Lillian Gilbreth: Partners for Life,* Edna Yost summarizes the situation, which in some marriages would have been fatal, that confronted Lillian.

> Actually it became a springboard for one of the most unusual marriages and, in the estimation of the two most intimately concerned, one of the happiest and most successful. The way of the marriage was primarily of the husband's inception and the wife's creative acquiescence. Doubtless its inception had some of its roots in the tie between Frank and his mother, and his unwillingness to incur the kind of break from her that is usually regarded as essential for

establishing an adult relationship with a wife.

> Doubtless her acquiescence had some of its
> roots in Lillian's tie to her own parents. Frank
> outlived his mother by only four years. The tie
> between them was deep and strong until the
> end and put an unusual degree of adjustment
> on Lillian's shoulders. She made the adjust-
> ment because she saw her husband as a most
> unusual man. He had almost no sense of per-
> sonal limitations and living with him helped
> her to discover her own limitations were
> sometimes of self-imposed origin.[26]

Both Frank and Lillian wanted a large family, but she was
surprised to hear that he wanted twelve children. She wasn't
dismayed by this; Lillian was the oldest of nine children. Her
background of playing second fiddle to her attractive, person-
able younger sister and her thoughts as a young woman that
she was not attractive to men probably helped her adapt to life
with her strong-willed husband. Biographer Edna Yost
observes the forces that were at work within Lillian:

> Romantically, blindly, unreservedly in love,
> she trusted this man, with his unusual philoso-
> phy of the high value of work. She had faith
> that he would, as he promised, help her to
> achieve a continuing intellectual development.
> To have him feel as he assuredly did about a
> woman's work and a woman's mind was a ful-
> fillment beyond her wildest dreams....
>
> She withheld nothing—she gave to the limit of
> her being. For love's sake she ran the risk of

losing her life in his. Without his fundamental bigness she might have been lost. But the miracle happened—a miracle that has happened in the modern world all too rarely. It will happen often when more people of both sexes understand more of the truth about love, and that only when one dares to lose his [or her] life can he [or she] truly find it.[27]

## Cheaper by the Dozen

In addition to their busy careers, Lillian and Frank raised twelve children, one of whom died in childhood. In 1948, two of their children, Frank Gilbreth, Jr., and Ernestine Gilbreth Carey, published the story of their family in *Cheaper by the Dozen,* which was made into a movie.

Frank was accused by his friends as having more children than he could keep track of. In one of the family stories, Lillian was out of town giving a lecture and left Frank in charge of their brood. On her return, she asked him how everything had gone in her absence. He responded, "Didn't have any trouble except with that one over there, but a spanking brought him into line." Lillian pointed out, "That's not one of ours, dear; he belongs next door."

No one in the family remembers this actually happening. They attribute it to the fact that the only thing Frank liked more than telling a story about Lillian was telling one about himself. However, the children remembered that two red-headed children lived next door, and all of the Gilbreth children were either redheads or blondes.

Frank applied his motion study concepts at home as well

as on his construction projects. He took motion pictures of the children washing dishes to eliminate movements and make them more efficient. He asked the children to bid on jobs around the house, such as painting the porch. The son or daughter who submitted the lowest sealed bid got the job and the associated spending money.

Frank buttoned his vest from the bottom up because it took only three seconds—from the top down took seven seconds. He installed process charts in the bathrooms for the children to initial in the morning after they had brushed their teeth, taken a bath, combed their hair, and made their bed. At night, the children initialed a worksheet after they had weighed themselves, completed their homework, washed their hands and face, and brushed their teeth. It was regimentation, but Frank thought that discipline was important in shepherding twelve offspring through their day.

## Frank and Lillian as Partners

Lillian was a quick study in learning the construction business. Sometimes her opinions differed from his, particularly on the people side of the business. He thought that workmen always wanted to do what he thought they should so; she realized that this wasn't always true. Occasionally, she became the teacher and he was the student. Edna Yost comments that:

> Frank could not easily accept Lillian's occasional role as teacher. He was ten years older and an aggressive dominating male. He had, too, the kind of ego that she would never develop. Plenty of times he told her tomorrow

what she taught him yesterday and insisted that she see and believe it. To realize how easily he learned was enough happiness for Lillian. To his eternal credit, he recognized the trait in himself and fought it, publicly and privately acknowledging what he got from her.[28]

Their work became a joint effort that wasn't divided into her contribution and his contribution; it was their effort. The contracting and construction aspects of the business didn't really appeal to her. The people side of the business interested her, and she was a vital contributor in documenting her husband's thoughts on management—the planning of work and the efficient completion of projects.

Their business grew substantially. They had construction sites around the country, including many on the West Coast. As their family grew, Frank disliked being away from home frequently. He conveyed these thoughts to Lillian in many "Dear Chum" letters.

In December 1907, Frank met Frederick Taylor, the "Father of Scientific Management." Taylor concentrated on time study and Frank specialized in motion study. Frank thought that if a job were done in its most efficient way, the time that it took would be at a minimum. Later, the two specialties merged into time and motion study.

Taylor, who was ten years older than Frank, became chief engineer for the Midvale Steel Company in the 1880s. He was imaginative and had a probing mind. While others worked to improve the technology of producing steel, Taylor strove to make the workers who produced the steel more efficient in doing their tasks.

Management training at the time was accomplished via apprenticeship programs. Taylor was the first to apply the inductive method to the challenges of managing a factory. His initial emphasis on time study was a means of reducing the pay of nonproducers. Eventually, he applied the inductive method to both the administration and the operation of a factory. He divided work into two distinct functions, planning and execution; also, he set finite, standardized tasks for all workers to allow the application of a bonus or a penalty to each worker's pay.

One of the differences in the outlook of Taylor and Frank was their viewpoint about unions. Taylor had had mainly negative experiences with unions of lower skilled workers; Frank had experienced principally positive experiences with unions of higher skilled workmen. A shortcoming of Taylor's landmark paper, "Shop Management," is that he advocated time study of existing methods. He didn't stress the improvement of those methods. Doing tasks more efficiently was the goal of Frank's motion study approach.

Although Lillian had three babies in the first three years of their marriage, she worked actively in the business, including climbing scaffolds when necessary. Frank's milestone book, *Bricklaying System,* was published in 1909, one year after he published *Concrete Construction.* In 1911, he published *Motion Study: A Method for Increasing the Efficiency of the Workman.* Lillian's help was vital to Frank in compiling and editing his thoughts in preparing the books for publication.

Lillian observed that Frank had a good relationship with his workers, and informally was using the little-understood principles of psychology as they existed at the time. She suggested combining these principles of psychology with the practice of management. Frank considered her to be "a very remarkable woman," who had moved from being his student / assistant to his junior partner and was moving up to even greater responsibility.

Edna Yost's description of their relationship at this stage cannot be improved upon:

> The experience of loving this man, with the inner attitudes she had brought to marriage, and of having that man accept her as the possessor of a good mind he expected her to use and develop, had a very wholesome effect upon her. She had used increasingly the qualities he called upon and developed as one can develop only in an atmosphere of both work and appreciation.
>
> As he had believed that nothing he wanted to do was impossible, he now believed it of her ... two fully cooperating human beings are each stronger than either would be alone. Now, when he wanted her to arrange the physical aspects of their life so that she might complete work for her Ph.D., she knew how greatly he would cooperate and was ready to undertake the work.[29]

In 1911, Frederick Taylor published his seminal work,

*The Principles of Scientific Management.* Although Taylor gave credit to others who contributed to the development of his principles, it was becoming apparent that he wasn't going to credit Frank as a contributor to the subject of motion study.

In his book and in a paper published in *Engineering* in London that was reprinted in the American Society of Mechanical Engineering *Transactions,* Taylor observed that "motion study has been going on in the United States with increasing volume." Taylor also observed that his colleague in time study, Sanford Thompson, was "perhaps the most experienced man in motion study and time study in the country."

In 1912, a difficult year for Frank and Lillian, the Gilbreth business was operating with financial stress because Frank didn't want to apply for additional loans and be controlled by bankers. Also that year, the two oldest daughters, Anne and Mary, contracted diphtheria at school. Six-year-old Anne was able to fight off the disease, but her younger sister succumbed. Mary's death devastated Frank and Lillian. After her death, both parents had difficulty talking about the loss of their daughter.

When she recovered from this unexpected blow, Lillian completed her doctoral dissertation, "The Psychology of Management," for the University of California at Berkeley. The University approved her dissertation, but required her to complete an additional year of resident study before awarding her Ph.D.

Lillian and Frank decided to have the dissertation published serially by the periodical, *Industrial Engineering.* In

1914, Sturgis and Walton were willing to publish it in book form—by L. M. Gilbreth as cited in *Industrial Engineering*— if the fact that the author was a woman was not publicized. When Frank was asked if L. M. Gilbreth was related to him, he responded, "Only by marriage."

Frank's next construction project was in Providence, Rhode Island, the home of Brown University. Brown offered a Ph.D. program in Applied Management that fit Lillian's needs precisely. She was now a full partner with Frank in developing scientific motion study methods. The move to Providence had the additional benefit of getting the children away from their home in Montclair, New Jersey, where their sister Mary had died.

With a family of six children, the Gilbreths had to establish a regimen that would permit Lillian to complete her studies while Frank spent long hours on his construction projects. They hired a housekeeper, a handyman, and a Pembroke College student who served as an au pair girl for the children. Frank's mother was in her late seventies but was in excellent health and helped with the household duties.

At Brown University, Lillian continued to develop the concept of micro-motion techniques and also studied about the elimination of fatigue. Fatigue in the workplace was mental as well as physical, and she sought ways of combining the psychological aspects with the concept of motion study. Both Lillian and Frank participated in a series of summer programs at Brown. In one of these sessions, Frank stated his lofty vision of American industry:

- efficiency in all work processes and operations
- the happiness of industry's human components at all
  levels, as such happiness can be achieved through the
  use of the highest qualifications for work each human
  being possesses and wishes to use
- an equable sharing of profits, not only in wages but in
  all that an industry should be in a community

Frank undertook assignments with companies in Europe, and he was returning from one of those jobs when Lillian received her Ph.D. from Brown University. The Gilbreths moved back to Montclair, New Jersey, after Lillian finished her doctoral studies.

In the United States, Frank and Lillian applied their motion study techniques at companies such as Cluett Peabody, Eastman Kodak, Pierce Arrow, and U.S. Rubber. Lillian usually accompanied Frank on the first plant visit for their projects when they were sizing up the task ahead. Gilbreth Associates had managers capable of directing projects, including their first employee, J. W. Buzzell; however, Lillian was Frank's only partner. In his letters to her at this time, his salutation was "Dear Boss" not "Dear Chum."

The Gilbreths believed that there were a maximum of seventeen elements to a complete motion cycle:

| | | |
|---|---|---|
| • Search | • Use | • Transport, empty |
| • Find | • Dissemble | • Wait, unavoidably |
| • Select | • Inspect | • Wait, avoidably |
| • Grasp | • Transport, loaded | • Rest, necessary for overcoming fatique |

- Position　　• Pre-position
　　　　　　　　for next operation
- Assemble　　• Release load　　• Plan

Frank volunteered for military service during World War I. He was commissioned a major and assigned to the Army Corps of Engineers at Ft. Sill, Oklahoma, where he helped to prepare fifty training films used in the field training of soldiers. His motion study background was used, for example, in documenting the steps "in the quick and easy assembly of a Browning Machine Gun." He developed severe uremic poisoning at Ft. Sill and, with the added complication of pneumonia, almost died. Lillian came down to the base hospital to be with him. Upon his recovery, he was discharged from the Army and rejoined Lillian at Gilbreth Associates.

An Honorary Membership in the Society of Industrial Engineering was bestowed upon Lillian in the spring of 1921 in Milwaukee. For the first time in his life, words failed Frank. He was so happy for her that no words came out when he was called upon to speak. The resulting applause rescued him. She claimed that the Honorary Membership was due to Frank's overstressing her contributions, but her own book, *Psychology of Management,* was highly regarded and frequently quoted.

In 1924, the Gilbreths planned to attend the World Power Conference in London and the International Management Congress in Prague. Early one morning, Frank prepared to travel to Manhattan to have their passports renewed. He called from the railroad station in Montclair to tell Lillian that he had forgotten to bring the passports with him. She left the telephone to look for them, and when she returned there was no one on the line. The police asked a neighbor to stop by and tell her that Frank had dropped dead in the telephone booth.

Lillian and the children were devastated. They were a close-knit family, and all of the children revered their father. According to his wishes, he had a simple funeral service with no music or flowers. The service had a military tone, and he was buried in his Army uniform. Lillian told her friends that "she had had more from her husband in twenty years of marriage than any other woman she had ever known had had in twice that time." She knew that her rich marriage with Frank would help her in the difficult times ahead.

## Lillian Alone

Several days later, Lillian sailed for Europe as Frank would have advised her to do. She attended the Power Conference in London and then traveled to Prague for the International Management Congress. She read the paper that they had prepared for him to read in Prague, chaired the session in which he was scheduled to preside, and was made an Honorary Member of the Masaryk Academy in his place. She controlled her emotions with difficulty as members of the Congress paid many tributes to her husband.

Upon her return home, she consulted with the eleven Gilbreth children about their future. Frank and Lillian had placed a priority on a college education for all of the children, and she intended to honor that plan. Lillian's mother invited

Lillian and the children to move in with her and to take advantage of the California educational system. However, consulting opportunities for Lillian were greater on the East Coast where she was better known.

Lillian delineated her goals for the future:

- Provide a home, a living, and love for the family
- Maintain Frank's work. Teach his ideals and techniques to younger people who will keep them alive and progressing
- Push forward cooperative research projects in the areas of his interests, especially the motion study aspects of problems affecting the health and efficiency of human beings in industry

Her first project was a request from Johnson & Johnson to establish a facility to train their employees in motion study techniques. This task meshed with an activity that she and Frank had planned to do anyway. She continued with Frank's ongoing projects and began work on a new assignment for R. H. Macy and Company. When she had spent the insurance money and the money received from selling their car, she had to borrow from her mother to help pay for living and school expenses. All of these loans were repaid in full.

Lillian faced significant challenges. At the age of forty-six, she had to venture out on her own without the backing and advice of her strong-willed husband. However, Lillian had inner strengths that she drew upon. She needed these strengths at a time when women were not universally accepted in industry.

Initially, she was faced with providing the necessary discipline for her teenage children, particularly her sons. Then she had to cope with providing for forty-four years of college education, four years for each of her eleven children. Their eleven bachelor degrees included three from the University of Michigan and two from Smith College.

In October 1930, with the country struggling with the Great Depression, Lillian was asked to head the women's unit of the President's Emergency Committee for Employment. She devised a plan to use women's clubs and other national organizations to conduct job surveys and to determine how to use the unemployed.

The chairman of the Committee for Employment credited Lillian with "conceiving a new method to apply to an old evil ... a brilliant conception and carried through with speed and skill." Following her success with this program, she was asked to serve with the President's Organization on Unemployment Relief.

In 1935, Lillian was invited by President Elliott of Purdue University and Dean Potter of its Engineering School to join the Purdue faculty. They offered her an appointment as Professor of Management that allowed her time for outside consulting. This appointment provided her with the opportunity of passing on the principles of motion study to younger people and gave her more employment stability than consulting provided during the Depression.

Initially, she was required to be away from Montclair, where her younger children were still in school, for three weeks out of every four. The Purdue experience was very rewarding for her; she retained her appointment there until her retirement in 1948. Lillian had always been healthy, and her health continued to be good as she grew older. She followed the physical exercise program that Frank devised for her use after the births of their children.

In 1931, Lillian was awarded the first Gilbreth Medal by the Society of Industrial Engineering "for distinguished contribution to management." She received many honors, including an honorary Master of Engineering degree from the University of Michigan and an appointment as the only woman delegate to the World Engineering Congress in Tokyo.

One of her greatest honors was awarded at an annual joint meeting of the American Society of Mechanical Engineers and the American Management Association: "To Dr. Lillian Moller Gilbreth, and to Dr. Frank B. Gilbreth posthumously ... the 1944 Gantt Medal, in recognition of their pioneer work in management and their development of the principles and techniques of motion study...."

Lillian was considered to be the First Lady of Engineering in her later years; Frank had trained her well. Together they made significant contributions to their field that were greater that either of them could have made individually. Frank and Lillian Gilbreth provide us with an outstanding example of the synergy of a man and a woman working together.

Queen Victoria and Prince Albert
Courtesy George Eastman House

## Chapter 5

## QUEEN VICTORIA AND PRINCE ALBERT

*"It was a the first stage in the development of a highly success-
ful royal team, which became known throughout Europe in the
midyears of the century. At first the queen was in the ascendant,
although she sometimes caught herself listening when she
should have been talking; then the pair were equal working
partners; but within three years Albert was the one who led,
while the Queen, living through a succession of pregnancies
which lasted into the next decade, was happy to sit back in won-
dering admiration before an ever-increasing number of brilliant works and achievements of statecraft performed by 'the
beloved one.'"[30]*

*E. E. P. Tisdall, Queen Victoria's Private Life*

Victoria was crowned Queen of England at the age of eighteen and initially relied heavily on the advice of her Prime Minister, Lord Melbourne. Melbourne was considerably older than she was, but they had a close working relationship that gave Victoria an opportunity to learn gradually how to deal with her responsibilities. After her marriage to Prince Albert of Saxe-Coberg-Gotha, her husband became a principal advisor. Victoria and Albert were married at a time when royal marriages were arranged to form alliances between countries. However, Victoria was sufficiently strong-willed to choose her mate.

Albert was autocratic by nature, and early in their marriage he chafed at having so little responsibility. When Victoria began to recognize the quality of the assistance that Albert could bring to the performance of her duties, she gave him additional responsibilities. He was a contributing force in England's assembly of an empire on which the "the sun never set" during Victoria's reign. Victoria and Albert were in love, and both gave a high priority to children and family. They are another outstanding example of the complementary strengths of a man and a woman.

**Victoria and Albert as a Team**

Victoria and Albert had two distinctly different personalities. She was outgoing and very willing to express her feelings. Victoria didn't represent the repressed human qualities that were considered to typify the "Victorian era." She loved Albert deeply and expressed her feelings to him openly. The queen enjoyed her home life and loved dancing, games, and the theatre.

Albert was an introverted, conservative man with reserved tastes. He was studious, hard-working, and serious. He enjoyed riding in the countryside and liked intellectual gatherings at which he had the opportunity to talk with artists and philosophers.

However, they had common interests, which helped to keep them close as a married couple. They both enjoyed dancing, music, and riding. Initially, Albert didn't like to dance, but he danced because his wife enjoyed it. He became a proficient and skilled dancer. In her younger years, Victoria didn't like to socialize with artists and thinkers, but Albert helped to expand her horizons. Albert regarded the composer Felix Mendelssohn highly and helped to sponsor Mendelssohn's contributions to the Romantic movement in music.

Victoria and Albert were a happy couple who were devoted to each other. The Prince's letters to his wife were always the words of a lover. When away from her, Albert repeatedly said that he longed for her presence and that he looked forward to being in her embrace.

The royal family expanded in November 1840 with the birth of the Princess Royal, "Vicky," who married the Crown Prince of Prussia in 1858 and became the mother of Emperor William II of Germany, the "Kaiser" during World War I. The Prince of Wales (Edward VII) was born in 1841; followed in 1843 by Princess Alice, who became the grand duchess of Hesse; in 1844 by Prince Alfred, later the Duke of Edinburgh and the Duke of Saxe-Coburg-Gotha; Princess Helena in 1846; in 1848 Princess Louise (Duchess of Argyll); in 1850 Prince Arthur (Duke of Connaught); in 1853 Prince Leopold (Duke of Albany); and in 1857 Princess Beatrice (who married Prince Henry of Battenberg).

Albert spent more time in the children's nursery than his wife did. He checked on the children each night and returned at eight o'clock in the morning to ensure that all were well. Then he would carry one of the younger children in to see Victoria. However, the Queen wasn't very interested in her children during their first six months. Albert was also good at calming his children's sudden outbursts of temper. He was more effective at this than their governesses and nurses. However, when the children entered the early teens and developed opinions of their own, he was less effective in dealing with them.

Victoria by nature was a passionate woman. When told by her doctor after the birth of Beatrice that she could have no more babies, she replied, "Oh doctor, can I have no more fun in bed?"[31] Biographer Dorothy Thompson in *Queen Victoria: The Woman, the Monarchy, and the People* observed, "If the stereotypical Victorian woman was well-mannered, self-effacing, demure, and devoid of passion, Queen Victoria was so far from the stereotype as to almost be the opposite."[32]

## Victoria's Early Life

Victoria, Queen of the United Kingdom of Great Britain and Ireland, Empress of India, was born at Kensington Palace on

May 24, 1819. She was the only child of Edward, the Duke of Kent, and Princess Victoria Mary Louisa of Saxe-Coburg-Gotha. Victoria's father died when she was eight months old. Leopold, her mother's brother, who had been the husband of Princess Charlotte and thus Prince Consort of England, became Victoria's surrogate father. In 1831, Leopold left England to become the first King of Belgium.

Leopold was responsible for the general character of Victoria's education and continued to be her advisor after he moved to Belgium. On Leopold's death, his niece entered into her journal that he had been "ever as a father" to her.

When Victoria was five years old, Fräulein (later Baroness) Louise Lehzen, a native of Coburg, became her governess. Baroness Lehzen was the main influence on young Victoria's life, even surpassing the influence of her mother, the Duchess of Kent. Since Victoria had a Coburg mother, a Coburg guardian-uncle, and a Coburg governess, she considered herself to be more a member of the House of Coburg than the House of Hanover. She grew up isolated from the surviving members of her father's family—her uncles King George IV and the Duke of Clarence, who subsequently became King William IV.

The fact that she would become queen was withheld from Victoria until she was twelve years old. When told of her future, she said, "I will be good." Her uncle, King George IV, died on June 20, 1837, and Victoria became Queen Victoria at the age of eighteen. Her subjects were impressed by the poise and reserve of young Victoria while the oaths were administered by the Lord Chancellor at her coronation ceremony on June 18, 1838. The United Kingdom looked forward to the rule of their youthful queen.

Victoria was fortunate that Lord Melbourne was Prime Minister when she became Queen. The bachelor in his late fifties became her mentor and closest advisor. Melbourne was tactful in his instruction of the new sovereign, and their working relationship evolved into what many viewed as a "romantic friendship."

Leopold's long-term plan was for Victoria to marry his nephew, Prince Albert, the second-oldest son of the Duke of Saxe-Coburg-Gotha. Leopold was aided in implementing this plan by his advisor, Baron Stockmar, who became an advisor to Albert. Albert, who was the same age as Victoria, was coached by the capable Stockmar—a doctor of medicine in his first career. Prince Albert traveled to London and met Victoria before her coronation. The plan appeared to be proceeding favorably until Victoria told Lord Melbourne that she didn't see why she should ever marry.

## Albert's Early Years

Francis Charles Augustus Albert Emmanuel, the second son of Duke Ernest of Saxe-Coburg-Gotha and his first wife, Princess Louise of Saxe-Gotha-Altenburg, was born at Rosenau on August 26, 1819. Prince Albert's father's sister married the Duke of Kent. The Duchess of Kent was Queen Victoria's mother; therefore, Victoria and Albert were first cousins.

Prince Albert's parents separated in 1824, when he was five years old. They divorced the following year, and Princess Louise and Duke Ernest both remarried. Duke Ernest was a kind, understanding father who believed in discipline for his sons. Young Albert's letters to his father and to his mother when he was away from home show his affection for his parents. Albert had fond memories of growing up in the Thüringerwald between Coburg and Gotha.

Albert and his older brother, Ernest, were tutored at home and educated at the University of Bonn. Prince Albert studied natural science, political economy, and philosophy at the University. He enjoyed music and painting and excelled in gymnastics and in fencing.

When Prince Albert moved to England, the London press gave him three nicknames: the "pauper prince," "lovely Albert," and the "German professor." None of the nicknames were complimentary. He dressed like a dandy, and he looked foreign to them. The press called him the pauper prince because he was the second son of the duke of a small principality and "lovely Albert" because that was what Queen Victoria called him. He was called the "German professor" because he was most at ease while discussing some academic, artistic, or scientific topic.

## Victoria's and Albert's Early Marriage Years

Albert visited London a second time in October, 1839, and completely captivated Great Britain's young queen. Victoria thought that Albert was "extremely handsome." She proposed to him, and their engagement was announced before he returned home. Victoria wrote to her uncle, King Leopold I of Belgium, to thank him for the "prospect of great happiness you have contributed to give me in the person of dear Albert. He possesses every quality that could be desired to render me perfectly happy."

Victoria and Albert were married on February 10, 1840, at the chapel-royal, St. James. Victoria described driving away from the chapel in a carriage "Albert and I alone which was *so delightful.*" Victoria was a young woman in love. She wrote in her journal that "his excessive love and affection gave me feelings of heavenly love and happiness I never could have hoped for before ... his beauty, his sweetness and gentleness—really how can I ever be thankful enough to have such a husband."

Albert was immediately confronted with a dilemma. The British government didn't know what to call him, since there was no precedent for his position. They settled on the title "Prince Consort" but reduced the expected amount of his annuity from £50,000 to £30,000. A greater dilemma was that although Victoria was devoted to him as a wife, she didn't want to relinquish any of her duties to him or to use him as an advisor. Eventually, he worked his way into her confidence, but this occurred gradually over a long period of time.

Early in their marriage, Albert was frustrated by the lack of an outlet for his energies. He was uncomfortable with the purposelessness of his existence as the Prince Consort. Since he was not allowed to participate in statecraft, he decided to reorganize Buckingham Palace, which had become a model of inefficiency, mismanagement, and waste.

Household functions had become cumbersome due to a division of labor across three departments and duplication of assigned tasks. For example, the Office of Woods and Forests was responsible for washing windows on the outside, and the Lord Chamberlain's department washed windows on the inside. Since they washed windows at different times, the windows were always dirty. Another example of poor organization of work was that fireplace fires were prepared by the Lord Steward's department, but lighting the fires was the responsibility of the Lord Chamberlain. Albert corrected these organizational problems, and his increases in efficiency reduced the household expenses.

## Albert Assumes Additional Duties

Eventually, an act of nature eased Albert into the decision-making process at the palace; Victoria became pregnant. The Privy Council remembered that Princess Charlotte had died in childbirth, and they were concerned that if Victoria died her heir to the throne would need a regent. Tradition dictated that the regent would be Albert; therefore, it was sensible to prepare Albert for this situation should tragedy occur.

In September 1840, Albert became a member of the Privy Council and began to study England's constitution and laws. He started to take on many of the administrative tasks, and Victoria realized that he did them well. Ministers who earlier had hesitated to allow him to participate in the government began to recognize his ability and to appreciate his intelligence.

Victoria was fortunate that Albert had no personal interest in power for himself. In fact, his personal goals were to "sink his own individual existence in that of his wife—to aim at no power by himself, or for himself ... but making his position entirely a part of the Queen's continually and anxiously to watch every part of the public business, in order to be able to advise and assist her any moment in any of the multifarious and difficult questions brought before her...."

Albert realized that England faced serious issues at home. During the 1830s, dramatic social changes had occurred due to fast-paced industrial development. The distance grew between the rich and the poor and between the owner / managers and the workers. Benjamin Disraeli later referred to the differences between the classes as the "two nations."

Albert convinced the Queen to increase her involvement in foreign affairs in addition to her interest in domestic affairs. Victoria proposed that Albert should have access to all foreign dispatches, and the Prime Minister agreed. However, Albert wasn't satisfied to merely review the dispatches. He was consulted on behalf of the Queen on any action taken by the government outside of Great Britain. Ultimately, she came to regard foreign affairs to be within her area of responsibility as sovereign.

Victoria began to announce the decisions of the crown with the plural "we" instead of the singular "I." Albert became so closely identified with his wife that they were regarded as one person. Victoria had the title of Queen, but Albert performed many of her duties. Many in the government considered him as King for all practical purposes.

## Albert's Contributions to the Monarchy

In the general election of 1841, Robert Peel replaced Lord Melbourne as Prime Minister. Peel had served briefly as Prime Minister previously, but he had resigned due to differences with Queen Victoria. Albert worked well with Peel, and eventually he smoothed the way for a good working relationship between the new Prime Minister and the Queen. Peel's effectiveness as a leader and statesman eventually earned Victoria's respect. Albert became the Queen's partner in politics, and, because of his intellect, industry, and good judgment, eventually became her principal advisor.

Albert was fascinated by Britain's industrialization and with each new advance in technology. He convinced Victoria to have a Great Exhibition in London in 1851 to showcase England's advancements not only in science and technology but also in the arts. All of the industrialized nations were invited to participate and to display the results of their accomplishments.

A large palace made of glass was built in Hyde Park. The "crystal palace" housed on 26 acres 14,000 exhibits from around the world. Exhibits were divided into four areas of interest: raw material, machinery and mechanical inventions, manufactures, and sculpture and art. The intent of the exhibition was to highlight the ingenuity of man and to preview the prospects of the coming new age.

Initially, neither the House of Commons nor the House of Lords was in favor of the exhibition. They were concerned about the "rogues and revolutionists" that it would bring to England. It was successful beyond anyone's dreams, particularly due to the good planning and hard work of Albert. The proceeds of over £150,000 from the Exhibition were used to buy land in Kensington upon which to build educational institutions and museums, such as the Imperial College, the Royal College of Music, the Natural History Museum, the Science Museum, and the Victoria and Albert Museum.

Albert took his duties to the crown seriously and worked long hours that included handling many administrative tasks that he could've delegated. His health began to suffer, and his appearance became haggard. Albert was virtually working himself to death. He suffered from insomnia and rheumatism. Their oldest son, whom they called Bertie, became involved in a scandal at Cambridge University with an actress. This incident upset Albert; he visited his son to try to reduce the unfavorable publicity on the incident.

At about that time, Albert became involved with the *Trent* affair, in which a British ship was seized by a U.S. man-of-war. Two Southern envoys to Great Britain were seized by a Northern warship. The relationship between America and Great Britain had become strained as the United States headed for civil war. This incident required sensitive handling, and Albert felt that he had to participate directly in resolving the ill will between the two countries.

After the resolution of the *Trent* affair, Albert's health began to fail. He surprised Victoria by saying that if he became gravely ill, he wouldn't fight to stay alive. Doctors diagnosed typhoid fever, the same illness that had recently taken the life of the Spanish royal family. In his weakened condition, Albert was unable to fight off the disease. He died on December 14, 1861, at the age of forty-one. Victoria was devastated; doctors had to administer a sedative to her.

**Victoria Without Albert**

Victoria plunged into an extended period of grief. This sudden shock affected her dramatically. She became inactive and withdrawn. She talked about her own death. Victoria ensured that Albert's name would be immortalized by the naming of the Albert Medal in 1866 in reward for gallantry in saving life, of Albert Hall in 1867, and of the Albert Memorial in London in 1876.

Victoria realized immediately how much she had relied on Albert in ruling the kingdom. Initially, she wouldn't speak directly with her ministers. She used Princess Alice as an intermediary. She emerged from her withdrawal from society in 1864, but her energy didn't began to return until 1866.

Benjamin Disraeli became Chancellor of the Exchequer and leader of the House of Commons that year and began to work directly with the queen. Victoria became Empress of India while Disraeli was Prime Minister.

Queen Victoria died on January 22, 1901, at the age of eighty-one. She had restored majesty and respectability to the

British throne. During her reign, industrialization had become a dominant factor in the economy. She had been Queen of Great Britain for over sixty-four years. Upon her death, the Victorian age ended, and the Edwardian era began.

# Chapter 6

## ELIZABETH BARRETT AND ROBERT BROWNING

*"How do I love thee? Let me count the ways.*
*I love thee to the depth and breadth and height*
*My soul can reach, when feeling out of sight*
*For the ends of Being and ideal Grace.*
*I love thee to the level of every day's*
*Most quiet need, by sun and candle-light.*
*I love thee freely, as men strive for Right;*
*I love thee purely, as men turn from Praise.*
*I love thee with the passion put to use*
*In my old griefs, and with my childhood's faith.*
*I lived with a love I seemed to lose*
*With my lost saints,—I love thee with the breath,*
*Smiles, tears, of all my life!—and, if God choose,*
*I shall love thee better after death."*

*From Sonnets from the Portuguese by Elizabeth Barrett Browning*

Elizabeth Barrett's reputation as a poet exceeded that of Robert Browning when they met. She was an invalid who rarely left her room in her parents' home. Initially, they corresponded, and then Robert arranged their meeting through a mutual friend. Each had a strong respect for the other's poetry, and they found that they had much in common emotionally. Elizabeth's father had forbidden his sons and daughters to marry. Since Elizabeth was chronically ill, she wasn't concerned about this parental edict until she met Robert.

Her health improved as the love between them developed. They were married secretly and moved to Italy. Elizabeth was disowned by her father, but she had a small annuity on which to live. Robert's income was not sufficient to support them. They remained deeply in love and had an idyllic marriage. They had no serious arguments, and each was strongly supportive of the other's writing. In her opinion, she had not begun to live until she met Robert. Ultimately, with her advice and editing, Robert's poetry gained a wider acceptance than his earlier works, and her poetry was also improved by his advice and suggestions.

## Elizabeth's Early Life

Elizabeth Barrett, the oldest child of Edward Moulton Barrett and Mary Graham-Clarke Barrett, was born on March 6, 1806, in Durham, England. Edward Barrett was a wealthy merchant whose family owned a plantation in Jamaica. Elizabeth received no formal education, but she read widely, and, to a large extent, was self-educated. She learned Greek by participating in her brother Edward's lessons. Her first poems, including "The Battle of Marathon," were published when she was thirteen.

In 1832, the Barrett family moved to Devon and three years later moved to London. In 1838, they moved to 50 Wimpole Street, which was popularized in Rudolf Besier's play, "The Barretts of Wimpole Street." She published "The Serafim and Other Poems" that year and suffered a serious health problem that affected her respiratory system, which possibly was due to abscesses in the lungs. Her health deteriorated to the point that she was considered an invalid.

For health reasons, she was sent to Torquay, where her brother, Edward, drowned. Elizabeth and Edward had been close. Because he had accompanied her to Torquay, she considered herself to be a least partially responsible for his death. In 1841, she returned to London as a complete invalid. She spent her days reclining on a sofa and rarely left her room. She received few visitors and couldn't envision much of a future for herself. However, she wrote many letters and stayed current in the literary world by corresponding with many of the scholars and writers of the day.

In 1844, her reputation as a poet was enhanced by publishing a new book of poems that included "A Drama of Exile" (about the exile of Adam and Eve from Paradise), twenty-eight sonnets, some romantic ballads, and miscellaneous poems. These poems elevated her standing with the critics and brought her to the attention of a fellow poet, Robert Browning.

## Robert's Early Years

Robert Browning, the oldest child of Robert Browning, Sr., and Sarah Wiedemann Browning, was born at Camberwell, England, on May 7, 1812. Robert's sister, Sarianna, was born two years later. Robert Browning, Sr., was a bibliophile and a scholar who worked for the Bank of England for fifty years. Robert grew up in a home with thousands of books. He attended private schools in his neighborhood, but most of young Robert's education was received at home with his father serving as one of his tutors. His education was almost exclusively literary and musical.

Father and son were very close throughout their lives. Robert was also close with his mother, even to the extent of sharing illnesses with her when he was growing up. He frequently displayed his temper as a young man; his tolerant parents provided an environment that was "sheltered, enclosed, dependent." He lived at home until he married at the age of thirty-three.

When he was sixteen, Robert attended classes in Greek at London University and decided that poetry was to become his life's work. A generous father was willing to finance his son's writing. Robert was never bothered by financial problems; he was grateful to his father for his support.

When he was twenty-one, Robert published, anonymously, "Pauline, a Fragment of a Confession." Mr. W. J. Fox of *The Monthly Repository* gave it a favorable review, but it was not well-received by other critics. In later years, Robert was ashamed of this early work and destroyed all the copies that he could find. At this stage of his development as a poet, he was strongly influenced by Shelley.

For the next twelve years, he was a prolific author writing "Paracelsus," "Sordello," "Pippa Passes," "Bells and Pomengranates," and five plays—"Strafford," "King Victor and King Charles," "The Return of the Druses," "A Blot in the 'Scutcheon," and "Colombe's Birthday." "Strafford" and "A Blot in the 'Scutcheon," had very short runs on the stage, and his other plays weren't produced for the stage. He wasn't considered a successful playwright.

Robert had a full social life, and he had many literary friends including John Forster, the literary critic of *The Examiner.* Initially, Forster was the only critic to perceive the merit of "Paracelsus." Thomas Carlyle was a close friend over the course of their lifetimes. Robert had many women friends but had no close attachments with women. That was about to change.

## Elizabeth and Robert Discover Each Other

Elizabeth's passion was one of ambition and of wanting to break out of the shell that her illness had imposed on her. She didn't think of love and sexual passion, but she wanted to find another person with whom she could share poetic passion. When she read "Paracelsus," she suspected that Robert Browning might be that poet. Most of what she knew of Robert was from his poetry and her interpretation of it. She knew a few facts about Browning, the man, from her distant cousin, John Kenyon.

In late December 1844, Robert returned from a trip to Italy and read Elizabeth Barrett's "Poems," which had been published the preceding August. He admired her poetry and heard about her from his friend and her cousin, John Kenyon. Robert wrote to Elizabeth to tell her how much he enjoyed her poetry.

In his first letter to her, Robert said, "I love your verses with all my heart, dear Miss Barrett." He didn't attempt to analyze her poetry; he said that "into me it has gone, and part of me it has become, this great living poetry of yours, not a flower of which but took root and grew ... I do, as I say, love these books with all my heart—and I love you too."

Elizabeth replied that she was delighted with "the sympathy of a poet, and such a poet!" She asked him for criticisms of her writing and offered some comments on his efforts: "'Mist' is an infamous word for your kind of obscurity. You are never misty—not even in 'Sordello'—never vague. Your graver cuts deep sharp lines, always—and there is an extra-distinctness in your images and thoughts, from the midst of which, crossing each other infinitely, the general significance seems to escape."

They corresponded frequently. Over 600 of their letters survive, providing a wealth of personal information for biographers. In one of her letters to him, she offers her views on writing: "Like to write? Of course, of course I do. I seem to live while I write—it is life, for me. Why, what is to live? Not to eat and drink and breathe,—but to feel the life in you down all the fibers of being, passionately and joyfully. And thus, one lives in composition surely—not always—but when the wheel goes round and the process is uninterrupted."

Initially, their letters were about their craft, but soon the relationship deepened beyond friendship. On May 20, 1845, they met for the first time. After that meeting, Robert wrote to her concluding his letter with "I am proud and happy in your friendship—now and forever. May God bless you!" He followed that letter with one declaring his love. He was moving too fast for her. She responded, "You do not know what pain you give me by speaking so wildly ... you have said some intemperate things ... fancies,—which you will not say over again, nor unsay, but forget at once." He replied that she had misunderstood him; she accepted his explanation.

Robert's letters give the impression of a man attempting to control an overwhelming emotion. Her letters in response provide a recurring theme; she is unworthy, and she fears that she will injure him because her poor health will limit his social activity.

Elizabeth had another problem in addition to her health concerns. Her autocratic father refused to allow any of his children, neither daughters nor sons, to marry. No rational explanation exists for this behavior. Several biographers have conjectured that some African-American blood had entered into the family genealogy in Jamaica, and that Barrett didn't want it passed on to subsequent generations of the family.

Elizabeth, the oldest child in the family, had been left a modest legacy on which she could live. Her sisters, Henrietta and Arabel, did not have a comparable annual stipend. They were entirely dependent on their father for support, or on a husband if they chose to go against their father's wishes and marry. Henrietta married, but Arabel remained single and was always financially dependent upon her father.

Elizabeth continued to hold Robert off. She viewed him as the giver and herself as the taker; she felt that she wasn't good enough for him. Ultimately, Elizabeth and Robert acknowledged to each other that they were very much in love, and they began to plan their marriage. Only two months before their wedding, she told him that he would be better off if he left her.

They planned to be married in secret, and then to wait for a time when her father was away to leave for a honeymoon in Italy. Elizabeth told her sisters of her plans, but wouldn't allow them to attend the wedding ceremony because it would upset their father. She didn't tell her brothers or most of her close friends about her wedding plans.

The deception during the two months before their wedding upset Elizabeth. She was not used to being devious. "I am so nervous that my own footsteps startle me ... To hear the voice of my father and meet his eyes makes me shrink back— to talk to my brothers leaves my nerves trembling." They were married in St. Marylebone Parish Church on September 12, 1846. Elizabeth lived another week in her father's house before embarking for France en route to Italy. She said, "I did hate so, to have to take off the ring."

On September 19, accompanied by her maid, the Brownings left for Italy. Elizabeth had almost fifteen years of happy married life and creative professional life ahead of her. She gave birth to a son in 1849, and in 1861, after a flurry of loving kisses, died peacefully in Robert's arms.

Their letters provide a comprehensive look at the complexity of their relationship. They even corresponded when Robert was away on a short trip, for example, to find a place to stay for the summer away from the heat of Florence. Both correspondents were able to express their feelings superbly in writing. Thankfully, although Robert destroyed many of his other letters, their letters to each other have survived.

## How Elizabeth and Robert Supported Each Other's Work

While living at the Casa Guidi in Florence, after the birth of their son Wiedemann ("Pen"), Elizabeth showed Robert the poems that she had written during their courtship but had never let him read. She had traced their courtship from hesitation, doubt, and reservation to a happiness of love that was reciprocated. They were personal poems; she suspected that he would object to their being published.

To the contrary, Robert considered them to be among the best sonnets in the English language. "When Robert saw them he was much touched and pleased—and thinking highly of the poetry he did not let ... could not consent, he said, that they should be lost to my volumes [of 1850] and so we agreed to slip them in under some sort of veil, and after much consideration chose the 'Portuguese,'" The collection of forty-three sonnets was entitled "Sonnets from the Portuguese."

Robert completed two volumes of poetry entitled *Men*

*and Women* while living in Florence. At the same time, Elizabeth worked on *Aurora Leigh*, a long prose poem that she described as "the novel or romance I have been hankering after for so long." She described it to her brother George as "beyond question my best work."

In her prose poem, Elizabeth addresses the question of whether women can be happy with just their art or if they need men to feel fulfilled. She uses an intricate plot to tell her "thoroughly modern" story.

Elizabeth told her sister Arabel, "Robert and I work every day—he has a large volume of short poems which will be completed by the spring—and I have some four thousand, five hundred lines of mine—I am afraid six thousand lines will not finish it."[33] To protect their work schedule, they didn't receive visitors before three o'clock. Elizabeth wrote in the drawing room and Robert worked in the sitting room. The doors to the dining room in between these two rooms remained closed. She wrote in an armchair with her feet raised; he worked at a desk.

Although Elizabeth and Robert edited each other's completed work, they didn't review each other's daily effort nor did they discuss their work on a daily basis. Elizabeth, in particular, had strong feelings about this. She thought that no matter how close two people are to each other, that closeness shouldn't extend to their work. She said, "An artist must, I fancy, either find or make solitude to work in, if it is to be good work at all." Until her work was completed, she kept the details to herself.

The Brownings visited London to oversee the printing of Robert's *Men and Women*. Elizabeth pitched in and read the proofs as they came off the press. The effort was very exhausting for her, but she was convinced that this work would enhance her husband's reputation. Her own effort to complete *Aurora Leigh* was postponed.

*Men and Women* was successful initially; the first edition was sold out immediately, and American publishers requested the rights to reprint it. Elizabeth had helped Robert to be clearer in expressing his artistic feelings. Critics were no longer calling his work obscure. Elizabeth had also helped him to think less of financial concerns and to place more emphasis on writing poems. She considered *Men and Women* a brilliant collection and hoped that his genius would be acclaimed by his peers.

When Elizabeth completed *Aurora Leigh*, Robert made arrangements to have it published; in effect, he acted as her business manager. Both read the proofs and prepared the manuscript for the press. In order to do this, he discontinued the promotion of his last collection and postponed work on his next book of poems. Sales of *Men and Women* began to slip; the work was in need of additional promotion.

Robert took drawing and sculpting lessons in Florence. While they lived in Italy, he wasn't as dedicated to writing as Elizabeth was. Over the course of their fifteen-year marriage, his poetic output wasn't nearly as great as hers. Before their marriage, he had lived at home where his sister and his parents had ministered to his needs. He had no responsibilities that diverted him from writing. After he was married, he had to look after Elizabeth, whose health continued to be delicate.

Their son, Robert Wiedemann Browning ("Pen"), was born on March 9, 1849. Elizabeth was productive writing poetry while she was pregnant. She completed the first part of "Casa Guidi Windows" during her pregnancy. Early in their marriage, Robert learned from Elizabeth; her reputation was greater than his at that time. She encouraged him to concentrate on dramatic monologues in poetry and to give up playwriting. She was concerned that he wasn't measuring up to his potential because of his reduced productivity. He wasn't concerned; he looked upon it as a temporary situation.

After the birth of their son, Robert began work on a long poem entitled "Christmas Eve and Easter Day." Elizabeth was a strong influence on the choice of a theme for this work. She suggested that he write from the heart, not the head, and that he convey his own thoughts using a minimum of dramatic devices. She encouraged him to write about his hopes and fears, particularly those of a religious nature, in his poetry.

On January 1, 1852, Elizabeth was pleased to hear that Robert had made a New Year's resolution to write a poem every day. He began with "Love Among the Ruins," "Women and Roses," and "Childe Rolande." However, his writing wasn't sustained. They were staying in Paris at the time, and he resumed his contacts with society. Elizabeth encouraged this, even though she wasn't up to accompanying him. However, she experienced social activity vicariously through him and stayed current with the Paris social scene.

Attending social events provided an outlet for Robert at a time when Elizabeth's poor health restricted her mobility. However, talk continued to be an important ingredient in the couple's relationship. They knew that as long as they could be together and communicate freely, Elizabeth's delicate health wouldn't ruin their marriage. This openness extended to instances of minor disagreement. Elizabeth wrote to Robert's sister Sarianna that "the peculiarity of our relation is that even when he's displeased with me he thinks out loud and can't stop himself."

The Brownings' marriage was solid and enduring. The few disagreements that they had involved viewing some of their friends from different perspectives and Elizabeth's desire to keep their son in curls and frilly clothes until he was twelve years old. Elizabeth could learn from Robert about the nature of people, but she tended to stay with her own evaluation of friends.

Their main difference of opinion was Elizabeth's belief in spiritualism and in communicating with the dead in séances. They attended sessions with the seer Daniel Douglas Home. Robert was unconvinced of the value of séances; he wrote a spoof of spiritualism entitled "Mr. Sludge, the Medium."

Elizabeth and Robert retained their own identities. They continued to think independently and to be exciting conversationalists. Neither of them tried to convert the other to their image of a partner in marriage. Robert wrote to his brother-in-law George, "I shall only say that Ba [Elizabeth] and I know each other for a time and, I dare trust, eternity... —We differ

... as to spirit-rapping, we quarrel sometimes about politics, and estimate people's characters with enormous difference, but, in the main, we know each other, I say."[34]

## Elizabeth's Death and Her Place in History

Elizabeth's health deteriorated during the last three years of her life. When she appeared to be slipping away, the doctor was summoned. She appeared to be sleeping; Robert whispered in her ear, "Do you know me?" She murmured, "My Robert—my heavens, my beloved!" She kissed him repeatedly and said, "Our lives are held by God." He laid her head on the pillow. She tried to continue to kiss him but could no longer reach him, so she kissed her own hand and extended it to him.

Robert asked, "Are you comfortable?" She responded, "Beautiful." She began to fall asleep again, and Robert realized that she shouldn't be in a reclining position when a cough was coming. He raised her up to ease the cough. She began to cough up the phlegm but then stopped. Robert wasn't sure if she had fainted or fallen asleep. He saw her brow contract as though in pain and then relax. She looked very young. Their servant Annunciata, who realized that she was dead, said in Italian, "Her last gesture a kiss, her last thought of love."

Robert's friends expected him to break down completely after the loss of one so close to him. However, he remained in control, partly because Elizabeth had died so peacefully in his arms. Robert knew that his friends felt sorry for him for what he had lost. He was extremely grateful for the fifteen years that he and Elizabeth had together. He knew that she had more to give, but he appreciated the rare union that they had.

Friends were also concerned about Pen, who had been as close to his mother as a son and a mother can get. He, too, held up well and, in fact, helped to console his father. Robert told his sister, Sarianna, that Pen was "perfect to me."

Elizabeth's place in literary history is summarized by the essayist and poet, Alice Meynell:

> The place of Elizabeth Barrett Browning in English literature is high, if not on the summits. She had an original genius, a great heart, and an intellect that was, if not great, exceedingly active. She seldom has composure or repose, but it is not true that her poetry is purely emotional. It is full of abundant, and often overabundant thoughts. It is intellectually restless ... she "dashed" not by reason of feminine weakness, but as it were to prove her possession of masculine strength. Her gentler work, as in the *Sonnets from the Portuguese,* is beyond praise. There is in her poetic personality a glory of righteousness, of spirituality, and of ardor that makes her name a splendid one in the history of incomparable literature.[35]

Although Elizabeth was only fifty-five when she died, she accomplished the goals that she set as a young girl: to produce lasting poetry that made a significant contribution to her era. She influenced other poets, including Emily Dickinson, even before she died.

Elizabeth wasn't sure that marriage was for her; she knew that the goals of husband, home, and children, by themselves, weren't enough. To have found Robert to love and to have her love reciprocated was more that she had hoped for. Having a son at the age of forty-three added to her joy. She never stopped appreciating her good fortune to be poet, wife, and mother. Her remaining goal was for Robert to make the mark in poetry of which she knew he was capable.

## Life After Elizabeth

Robert and Pen left Florence on July 27, 1861. They arrived in London in September traveling by way of Paris and Saint-Malo. Robert lived in London for the next twenty-five years. He visited Italy, but he never returned to Florence.

Initially, he was lonely, but eventually he resumed his literary connections in society. He published *Dramatis Personae* in 1864, which led to his being lionized. In 1867, Oxford University awarded him a Master of Arts degree "by diploma," and Balliol College elected him an honorary fellow.

*The Ring and the Book,* generally regarded as his masterpiece, was published in four volumes in 1868-69. Elizabeth's dreams were at last realized when he was hailed as "a great dramatic poet." In *The Ring and the Book,* which was based on Guido Franceschini's court case in Florence, Browning told the story of a gruesome murder twelve times. He versified the arguments of the counsels for the prosecution and the defense as well as the gossip of the busybodies. The story was told with the detail of a court recorder.

Browning's father died in 1866, and his sister Sarianna moved in with him to run his household. Robert never remarried; however, he had many close women friends, including Annie Egerton Smith of the Liverpool *Mercury*. She accompanied him to many concerts in London. After her sudden death in 1877, he lost his interest in music.

In 1881, the Browning Society was formed by Dr. Furnival and Miss E. H. Hickey. Browning continued to receive honors: a LL.D degree from Cambridge University in 1879, the D.C.L. from Oxford University in 1882, and a LL.D degree from Edinburgh University in 1884. In 1886, he became foreign correspondent to the Royal Academy.

During his twenty-eight years as a widower, privacy was important to him. He destroyed all of the letters of his youth and all of the letters to his family. He couldn't destroy his wife's letters to him, nor could he destroy his letters to her. However, he wasn't sure what to do with them. He left them to his son to decide; Pen published them in 1899. Robert never ceased promoting Elizabeth's work. He realized that part of his popularity was the fact that he was the widower of Elizabeth Barrett Browning.

Pen settled in Venice, and Robert and Sarianna visited him there every year. At about five p.m. on December 12, 1889, while visiting Pen, Browning said to his nurse, "I feel much worse. I know that I must die." To Pen, he said, "I am dying. My dear boy, my dear boy." He became unconscious about eight p.m. Two hours later, Pen and Sarianna at his bedside saw a "violent heaving of his big chest" and then no more movement.

Browning's body was transported to London for burial in Westminster Abbey. It was proposed that Elizabeth's body should be disinterred from the cemetery in Florence and buried alongside her husband. However, Pen decided that her grave shouldn't be disturbed.

Biographer and critic Leslie Stephen provides an insight into Browning's poetry:

> He was little interested in the historical or "romantic" aspects of life. He takes his subjects from from a great variety of scenes and places—from ancient Greece, medieval Italy, and modern France and England; but the interest for him is not the picturesque surroundings, but of the human being who is to be found in all periods ... he is interested in the real comedy and tragedy of life.
>
> His problem is always to show what are the really noble elements which are eternally valuable in spite of failure to achieve tangible results ... he protests, though rather by implication than direct denunciation, against the utilitarian and materialistic view of life and finds the prime element in the instincts which guide and animate every character. When he is really inspired by sympathy for such emotions, he can make his most grotesque fancies and his most far-fetched analyses subservient to poetry of the highest order.

It can hardly be denied that his intellectual ingenuity often tempts him to deviate from his true function, and that his observations are not to be excused because they result from an excess, instead of a deficiency of intellectual acuteness. But the variety of his interests: aesthetic, philosophical and ethical—is astonishing, and his successes are poems which stand out as unique and unsurpassable in the literature of his time.[36]

Robert certainly lived up to Elizabeth's expectations. He wasn't very productive in writing poetry during their marriage, but he created a body of quality poetry in his later years. The Brownings strongly supported each other in their work. Each of them would have been a notable poet without the advice and help of the other; however, their individual work was enhanced by the suggestions and encouragement of the other. Other loving and working relationships may have equaled that of the Brownings, but few have been so well documented. They were indeed fortunate to have what they had, even if it was only for fifteen years.

Robert Browning,
painted by D.G. Rossetti, 1855

Elizabeth Barrett Browning,
portrait by Michele Gordigiani, 1858

Edith, Agnes, Samuel, Ethel, Florence, and Antoinette Blackwell
Courtesy Radcliffe College, Schlesinger Library

## Chapter 7

## ANTOINETTE BROWN & SAMUEL BLACKWELL

*"The prophet Joel is quoted as saying, 'And it shall come to pass in the last days, saith God, I will pour out my spirit upon all flesh; and your daughters shall prophesy, and your young men shall see visions, and your old men shall dream dreams, and on my handmaidens I will pour out in those days of my Spirit; and they shall prophesy....' In the eleventh chapter of First Corinthians we learn that females were accustomed to act as prophetesses in those days under direct sanction of the apostles. We have no reason to think it was therefore unlawful for women of that time to speak in church ... Again, when St. Paul says, 'I suffer not a woman to teach,' if we are to take this admonition literally, we should not even feel free to teach our own children."[37]*

*Antoinette Brown Blackwell*

Antoinette Brown was the first woman ordained as a minister in the United States. Achieving her goal to become a minister was an uphill struggle through her undergraduate and divinity school education at Oberlin College. Being a pioneer Congregationalist minister was difficult; she didn't consider marriage seriously until she reached a point of self-doubt in her career.

When Antoinette met Samuel Blackwell, she was too busy to be impressed by him. She was familiar with the high-achieving Blackwell family, because she stayed with them in Cincinnati on her speaking tours of the Midwest. Her college classmate, Lucy Stone, had married Samuel Blackwell's brother, Henry. Samuel was extremely supportive of Antoinette's ministry and of her tours on the lecture circuit. He backed her in her work, but his principal contributions were earning an income as a businessman to support the family, being her emotional ally, and caring for the children and the household to allow her time to travel and to write a series of books.

## Antoinette Brown—Early Life

Antoinette Louisa Brown, the seventh of ten children of Joseph Brown and Abigail Morse Brown, was born in Henrietta, New York, in May 1825. Antoinette indicated her interest in religion at an early age when she gave a spontaneous prayer to conclude a family prayer meeting at the age of eight. In the following year, she asked about joining the village Congregational Church, at a time when joining the

Church so young was rare.

The small Henrietta Church was a member of the liberal branch of the Congregational Church, which emphasized God's mercy and forgiveness in addition to human goodness and initiative. The orthodox branch of the Church believed that people were morally corrupt, sinful, and dependent upon an all-powerful God, who would condemn them to hell if they did not obey His word.

Antoinette decided that she wanted to be a minister while in her teens. No woman had been ordained as a minister; however, in the 1820s, a Methodist woman had attempted to preach in New York State, but had given in to public opposition. The Quakers, who considered all church members to be ministers, permitted women to speak at worship services, but women were not usually considered to be leaders of the church community.

Antoinette was active in her Henrietta Church and spoke frequently at prayer meetings, at which any church member was permitted to speak. She decided to attend the Oberlin Collegiate Institute in Ohio, where her brother, William, studied theology. Oberlin was the first U.S. college to admit women to take college courses with men. In the spring of 1846, she began her studies at Oberlin.

Oberlin had been founded in 1833 by ministers from New England and New York. By the time that Antoinette arrived, the College had developed its own ideology, which was a combination of liberal religion, practical training, and the politics of reform. The spiritual leader of the Oberlin community was professor of theology Charles Grandison Finney, who had impressed Antoinette's parents at a series of revival meetings in Rochester during the winter of 1831. He was a captivating speaker who advocated the dual responsibility of an individual's commitment to God and his or her working toward a better society. He suggested that this dual responsibility should be implemented by applying one's intellect and education to saving individual souls and to improving society. He became Antoinette's mentor.

## Antoinette and her Friend, Lucy Stone

Antoinette met Lucy Stone, who later became a leader of the Women's Rights Movement, at Oberlin. Lucy was a follower of the radical abolitionist, William Lloyd Garrison. She had enrolled at Oberlin specifically to learn public speaking skills to use in advocating women's rights and the abolition of slavery.

The women students at Oberlin discovered early that the college had no intention of training them as public speakers. They learned how to write, but they were "excused" from participation in discussions and debates. Oberlin President Asa Mahan wanted women to be taught how to speak as well as how to write, but he was outvoted by the faculty. The policy was apparently based on the words of St. Paul: "Let a woman learn in silence with all submissiveness."

In 1846-47, during Oberlin's winter break, Antoinette taught at a large private academy in Rochester, Michigan. The experience verified what she already knew: "God never made me for a school teacher." The headmaster encouraged Antoinette to give her first public speech. She spoke in the village church and was pleased that "it was fairly well received by the students and by the community."

Antoinette and Lucy became close friends and confidants despite their differences of opinion. Lucy was more radical on the subject of abolition; she had left the Congregational Church because it approved of slavery and was against women speaking in public. Antoinette was disappointed that her closest friend didn't agree with her goals.

> I told her of my intention to become a minis-
> ter. Her protest was most emphatic. She said,
> "You will never be allowed to do this. You will
> never be allowed to stand in a public pulpit nor
> to preach in a church, and certainly you can
> never be ordained." It was a long talk but we
> were no nearer to an agreement at the end than
> at the beginning. My final answer could only
> be, "I am going to do it."[38]

## Antoinette's Path to Ordination

Antoinette completed her undergraduate studies at Oberlin in the summer of 1847. She returned home to Henrietta and practiced her public speaking: "I go out into the barn and make the walls echo with my voice occasionally but the church stands on the green in such a way that I have too many auditors when I attempt to practice there. The barn is a good large one however and the sounds ring out merrily or did before father filled it full of hay."

Antoinette returned to Oberlin in the fall to study theology. She felt that she was called to this vocation, and she was motivated to use her intellect, her ability as a public speaker, and her interest in public reform. However, although Oberlin was committed to providing women with a general education, the only profession for which it formally prepared women was teaching. In the Theology Department, women were allowed to attend classes if their goal was self-improvement.

Antoinette was assigned to write essays on the passages in the Bible stating that women should not preach: "Let your women keep silence in the churches, for it is not permitted unto them to speak.... Let the women learn in silence with all subjection. I suffer not a woman to teach, nor to usurp authority over the man, but to be in silence." Antoinette found confirmation of her choice of a profession in the words of the prophet Joel: "And it shall come to pass in the last days, saith God, I will pour out my spirit upon all flesh; and your sons and daughters shall prophesy."

In her essay, Antoinette observed that St. Paul's suggestion that women should learn in silence had been misinterpreted. She suggested that St. Paul had only intended to caution against "excesses, irregularities, and unwarranted liberties" in public worship. Professor Asa Mahan selected her essay for publication in the Oberlin Quarterly Review.

In the last year of their studies, Oberlin theology students were allowed to preach in area churches, but not to perform any of the sacraments. Antoinette said: "They were willing to have me preach, but not to themselves endorse this as a principle.... They decided, after much discussion, that I must preach if I chose to do so on my own responsibility." Although she was not given official recognition, Antoinette spoke in small churches nearby, usually about the popular subject of temperance.

Upon completion of her theology studies, Antoinette chose not to be ordained at Oberlin. Not only did she think that it would be "a delicate thing" with Oberlin's difference of opinion on women ministers, but also she preferred the usual path of ordination by a local parish that wanted her as a pastor. She cited "an instinctive desire to be ordained in my own church, and a belief that I could one day in the future be ordained by my own denomination which was then the Orthodox Congregational."

Antoinette didn't participate in the graduation exercises. In later years, she observed: "We were not supposed to graduate, as at that time to have regularly graduated women from a theological school would have been an endorsement of their probable future careers." Antoinette's name didn't appear in the roll of the theological school class of 1850 until 1908.

In 1850, Antoinette attended the First National Women's Rights Convention in Worcester, Massachusetts, where she spoke to disprove the biblical argument that women shouldn't speak in public. At the Convention, she met Lucretia Mott and Elizabeth Cady Stanton, two of the organizers of the Seneca Falls Convention two years earlier. Antoinette was introduced to many men and women who were active in social reform. She maintained her contacts with those whom she met, but she thought that her cause would probably not be best served by working with organized groups.

Antoinette decided to earn her living as a public speaker as her friend, Lucy Stone, was doing. Before radio and television, the lecture circuit or lyceum was an important means of informing and entertaining people. Women speakers were usually paid less than men. Antoinette told the lyceum organizers that "my terms, from principle, are never less than the best prices received by the gentlemen of the particular association where I speak." She found the work to be satisfying, and she consistently received favorable reviews in the local newspapers.

Liberal ministers such as William Henry Channing and Samuel J. May invited Antoinette to preach in their churches. Her oldest brother, William, who had initially opposed her desire to preach, invited her to speak in his church in Andover, Massachusetts. She decided that it was time to pursue her calling, and she began actively to look for a church in need of a pastor.

### Ordination as the First Woman Minister in the U.S.

During one of her speaking tours across New York State, Antoinette visited South Butler, in Wayne County. The members of the small Congregational Church listened to her speak, and then invited her to become their pastor at an annual salary of $300. In the late spring of 1853, she moved to South Butler and began to give two sermons every Sunday, one of which was prepared and the other extemporaneous.

Antoinette's responsibilities included pastoral duties,

such as visiting the sick, and she felt suited to her role as minister. She observed: "My little parish was a miniature world in good and evil. To get humanity condensed into so small a compass that you can study each individual member opens a new chapter of experience. It makes one thoughtful and rolls upon the spirit a burden of deep responsibility."

Antoinette's friend, Lucy Stone, met Henry Blackwell, brother of the pioneer doctor, Elizabeth Blackwell, at an abolitionist meeting. Henry fell in love with Lucy and immediately began to court her. Lucy met Henry's older brother, Samuel, and suggested that he visit Antoinette on one of his business trips. The Blackwell brothers were business partners in Cincinnati. Samuel called on Antoinette while en route to Boston. Samuel "enjoyed the visit exceedingly." Antoinette observed that "he stayed perhaps a half a day and had a pleasant visit.... He was not handsome." She was preoccupied with her church duties.

Antoinette's congregation was pleased with her work, and the governing body decided to proceed with her ordination. She already administered the sacraments, but the ceremony would provide public recognition of her ministry. Reverend Luther Lee, a minister from nearby Syracuse whom Antoinette knew from abolitionist meetings, agreed to preach the ordination sermon.

Reverend Lee based his sermon on the text, "There is neither male nor female; for ye are all one in Christ Jesus." He said: "... in the Church, of which Christ is the only head, males and females possess equal rights and privileges; here there is no difference.... I cannot see how the test can be explained so as to exclude females from any right, office, work, privilege, or immunity which males enjoy, hold or perform." He concluded by saying: "All we are here to do, and all we expect to do, is, in due form, and by a solemn and impressive service, to subscribe our testimony to the fact that in our belief, our sister in Christ, Antoinette L. Brown, is one of the ministers of the New Covenant, authorized, qualified, and called of God to preach the gospel of His Son Jesus Christ."

During the winter of 1854, Antoinette's duties weighed heavily upon her. Her job was a difficult one, and her responsibilities began to cause her emotional strain. A minister's functions were many and varied. She was expected to be tolerant and understanding, but, at other times, authoritative and judgmental. It was difficult for her to be a "father" figure. Her role would have been easier if she had the support of her friends and associates. However, Susan B. Anthony, Elizabeth Cady Stanton, and Lucy Stone all disapproved of her church affiliation. They did not perceive Antoinette's ministerial duties as a contribution to affecting change in women's status.

Antoinette felt isolated:

> It was practically ten years after my ordination before any other woman known to the public was ordained. It was therefore doubly hard for me—a young woman still in her twenties—to adapt myself to the rather curious relationship I must sustain either to home conditions or to those of a pastorate. Personally this was more

of an emotional strain than the enduring of any opposition that ever came to me as a public speaker or teacher.[39]

This isolation began to affect her in a serious way. She began to question her faith, particularly the emphasis on being condemned to eternal damnation unless saved by a stern God, as espoused by some of her congregation. She was motivated more by Charles Grandison Finney's teachings that stressed human goodness and striving to approach moral perfection. In July 1854, overcome by mental conflict and nervous exhaustion, she returned home to Henrietta to rest.

## Antoinette's and Samuel's Relationship

Samuel Blackwell was one of the individuals who helped Antoinette find herself during this difficult time. He provided comfort and support and helped her to re-evaluate her religious beliefs:

> In the midst of the blackness of darkness which was around me more or less that year in New York, Mr. Blackwell's optimism and the fact that he was passing through a very similar experience to my own from the orthodoxy of his early training and his early years, into a more sanguine religious phase than my own, enabled him to become to me a present help in time of trouble.[40]

Because he was only two years older than she was, Samuel became closer to her than her other mentors, including

William Henry Channing and Gerrit Smith, who were much older.

Antoinette stayed with the Blackwell family when she was in Cincinnati on the lecture circuit. Samuel's five sisters were all achievers: Elizabeth and Emily became doctors, Ellen and Marian were active in the Women's Rights Movement and other reform efforts, and Anna, who lived at the transcendentalist commune at Brook Farm for a while, was a newspaper reporter in Paris. Samuel was used to active women.

In late 1854, Lucy Stone agreed to marry Henry Blackwell if he would agree to devote his efforts to women's rights. Perhaps motivated by his brother's action, Samuel proposed to Antoinette about the same time. Antoinette hesitated, but she considered some of the women that she knew—such as Lucretia Mott—who had children, husbands, and homes, in addition to careers.

Later, Antoinette observed, "... when the early faith seemed wholly lost and the new and stronger belief not yet obtained, there seemed no good reason for not accepting the love and help of a good man and the woman's appreciation of all else that this implied." After their marriage, she was known as Reverend Antoinette L. B. Blackwell.

In 1850, Antoinette had written to her friend, Lucy Stone, that if she married "the matrimonial alliance would have to be placed on a different basis than the common." It was different in that Samuel wasn't a typical husband for his time. He shared in the work around the home willingly and without question. Later, Antoinette wrote: "Mr. Blackwell, who was engaged in business and might have fewer hours to give to home duties, declared himself more than willing to help me with home duties. This promise he kept for almost fifty years." "Home duties" included taking care of their five daughters.

Antoinette stated her vision of men's and women's work; it extended well beyond sharing the work around the house. In her essay, "Social Progress," in *Studies in General Science,* she envisioned men and women sharing both household chores and work outside the home for pay:

> When we become nobler as individuals, we shall find better modes of co-working for mutual assistance; for the best good of one is the best good of all. Woman must become a broader and more rational worker; more self-forgetting, remembering the well-being of the whole community; while man must equally learn that charity begins with the necessary, unending, small details of home and its inmates.

Later, she expanded on her vision:

> Wife and husband could be mutual helpers with admirable effect. Let her take his place in garden or field or workshop an hour or two daily, learning to breathe more strongly, and exercising fresh muscles in soul and body. To him baby-tending and bread-making would be most humanizing in their influence, all parties gaining an assured benefit.... We need a gener-

al reconstruction in the division of labor. Let
no woman give all her time to household
duties, but require nearly all women, and all
men also, since they belong to the household,
to bear some of the common household bur-
dens.[41]

Early in their marriage, Samuel worked in an office while
making real estate investments in his spare time that he hoped
would lead to providing an income for the family and allowing him time to write. In 1871, he gave up his office job and
supervised building and selling homes, which permitted him
to work at home. Their plan seems to have worked. Antoinette
wrote:

> ... the plan worked extremely well. Houses
> were built and sold and we both did a great
> deal of writing.... Mr. Blackwell wrote poems
> and articles for the press on topics of the day....
> I had published one or two books and was still
> much absorbed with the writing and the study
> necessitated while still speaking in public
> occasionally as opportunity offered and
> attending various conventions as in the older
> days.[42]

The Blackwells were helped in their plan by hiring ser-
vants to do some of the housework, including cooking and
housecleaning as well as taking care of the young Blackwells.
When the children were older, they had a governess. The care
of the children was shared by Antoinette, Samuel, and the
governess. Samuel was devoted to his children to an extent

that even surprised Antoinette: "He was both father and mother. The children were always more enthusiastic over what he did for them than what I did—it was so unusual for a father to be so motherly."

Antoinette's first large published work was *Studies in General Science*, a collection of essays. In 1875, her second work, *The Sexes Throughout Nature*, a compilation of essays first published in periodicals, was published. In 1876, she published *The Physical Basis of Immortality*, which was a synthesis of her philosophy. *The Philosophy of Individuality, or the One and the Many*, was published in 1893. Her last two books, *The Making of the Universe* and *The Social Side of Mind and Action* were published in 1914 and 1915.

Antoinette was drawn to the Unitarian Church. Samuel Blackwell and three of his sisters had already joined the Unitarians. In the spring of 1878, she joined the Unitarian Fellowship and asked to be recognized as a minister. In the fall of 1878, the Committee on Fellowship of the American Unitarian Association acknowledged her as a minister.

In 1879, Oberlin College recognized Antoinette's status by awarding her an "honorary" Master of Arts degree, the degree that she had earned during three years of study in the theological department. One change from her studies thirty years previously was that she no longer stood alone as woman minister. In 1864, Olympia Brown, motivated by Antoinette's talk to her class at Antioch College, was ordained as a Universalist minister. By 1880, almost 200 women were recognized as ministers, and many held full-time pastoral jobs.

In addition to her participation in the Women's Rights Movement, Antoinette was also active in the Association for the Advancement of Women and the American Association for the Advancement of Science. She didn't have the responsibility of a congregation for decades, but Antoinette considered herself to be a "minister emeritus" during her later years.

## Life Without Samuel

Samuel had two operations during the summer of 1901. Antoinette took care of him while he recovered. However, after a partial recovery, Samuel had a series of strokes and died in late October. After his death, Antoinette told Alice Stone Blackwell that Samuel "was always ready to do everything in his power to help me in my public work and to give me money for long journeys." However, she felt that Samuel was "just a little too diffident about pushing his own fortunes, even properly ... for himself and also for me."

Antoinette admitted that:

> [This diffidence is the] only respect in which I have felt a little freer since he was gone, because although I was never good at pushing I could do things that would have offended his taste. I think that we should never seek praise, but if people want to do things for you, let them, if there is no harm in it. He believed more in woman's work than I did, if possible, yet if I was to lecture on suffrage where I should have everybody against me he did not like me to be criticized and would rather I went somewhere else.[43]

In June, 1908, Antoinette was invited to Oberlin College to receive an honorary Doctor of Divinity degree. In introducing Antoinette to Oberlin President Henry Churchill King at the commencement ceremony, Dr. Charles Wager addressed the audience:

> It is appropriate for the institution that was the first to provide for higher education of women to honor, at its seventy-fifth anniversary, a woman who has eminently justified that daring innovation, a woman who was one of the first two in America to complete a course in divinity, who as preacher, as pastor, as writer, as the champion of more than one good cause, has in the past conferred honor upon her Alma Mater, and who today confers upon it no less honor by an old age as lovely as it is venerable.[44]

The Susan B. Anthony Amendment granting women the right to vote was ratified in 1920, and Antoinette voted in the national election that year. Her health began to fail during the spring and summer of 1921. She was at peace with herself; she was ready for death and looked upon it as a reunion with Samuel and all of the loved ones who had predeceased her. In late November 1921, at the age of ninety-seven, Reverend Antoinette L. B. Blackwell, the first woman minister, died in her sleep.

James and Lucretia Mott
Daguerreotype by Langenheim ca. 1842
Courtesy Smith College, Sophia Smith Collection

# Chapter 8

## LUCRETIA AND JAMES MOTT

*"Our [Lucretia's and James'] independence is equal, our dependence mutual, and our obligations reciprocal ... I owe the happiness of my own wedded life to the fact that my husband and I have always shared a deep interest in the sacred cause of wronged humanity."*[45]

*Lucretia Mott*

Lucretia Mott was the elder stateswomen of the Women's Rights Movement and the mentor of many of its leaders, particularly Elizabeth Cady Stanton. From her early experiences in Quaker meetings, Lucretia was used to thinking and speaking for herself. When Lucretia told Elizabeth Cady Stanton that she had as much right to think, write, and speak out as any man, the younger woman's eyes were opened.

James Mott shared his wife's interests and supported her efforts in the antislavery movement and the Women's Rights Movement. They functioned as a team. She was the better public speaker, but sometimes he had to do the speaking because on many occasions women were not permitted to speak in public—for example, at conventions. In fact, James Mott presided over the opening of the first Women's Rights Convention on July 19-20, 1848, in Seneca Falls, for that reason. Lucretia's achievements were orders of magnitude greater than they would've been without the help of her husband.

## Lucretia Coffin—Early Life

Lucretia Coffin Mott was born to Thomas Coffin and Anna Folger Coffin in Nantucket on January 3, 1793. Three factors shaped her early life: being born into a Quaker family; growing up with the hardy, independent, and self-reliant people of Nantucket; and having a father who believed in educating his daughters. The Quakers gave women virtual equality with men, permitted them to speak at Quaker meetings, and allowed them to become ministers. Lucretia Mott was accustomed to speaking in public; she became a minister in her twenties and was an accomplished speaker by the time she became active in the antislavery movement.

When Thomas Coffin, a whaler, was away on his sailing vessel, Anna Coffin ran their shop, kept the accounts, and made buying trips to Boston. Lucretia was used to seeing women in positions of responsibility on the Island. In 1804, the Coffin family moved to Boston and then eventually moved to Philadelphia, the hub of Quaker life.

After completing elementary school at the age of thirteen, Lucretia was enrolled in Nine Partners boarding school, an advanced Quaker academy near Poughkeepsie. The strong-willed Lucretia occasionally rebelled at the severity of the discipline. She could endure punishment for herself easier than she could tolerate it being inflicted on her classmates. The school building was divided into a "boys" side and a "girls" side, and boys and girls were not permitted to talk with one another. When a boy with whom she was friendly was confined to a closet on a diet of bread and water, Lucretia went to the boys' side of the school building to take additional food to him.

## Lucretia and James Meet and Marry

Lucretia received excellent grades at Nine Partners school, and, after graduating, she taught at the school. She met and fell in love with James Mott, who also taught at Nine Partners. In many ways, they were a contrast. She was short and dark-complected; he was tall and light-complected. She was open, bubbly, and optimistic; he was quiet and tended to be serious and somewhat pessimistic. She was perceived as a warm and friendly person; he was considered to be introverted and cold.

Lucretia considered his seriousness and reliability to be strengths on which she could lean. Her enthusiasm made James feel more alive, and he admired her ability to frame her thoughts and express them in ways that he couldn't. As a team, Lucretia's liveliness and sense of purpose stirred their actions.

Lucretia Coffin and James Mott were married on April 4, 1811, in Philadelphia, where James Mott had accepted a position in his father-in-law's business. Lucretia and James had a strong, loving marriage. Lucretia's and James' strengths were complementary. They participated in the same causes, but there was no rivalry between them. She was the talented leader and change agent; he chaired the meetings and generated the required letters and petitions to promote the activities in which they participated. She was more well-known than he was, but, supported by their deep love for each other, they considered themselves to be equal partners.

James might have become more famous if he hadn't been in Lucretia's shadow. Their few enemies called him Mr. Lucretia Mott; the Motts' large personalities didn't let it concern them. James' support allowed Lucretia to channel her drive and energy to constructive causes that gave them both a feeling of accomplishment.

Lucretia became a hard-working, nineteenth-century

housewife and mother of six children. She also became known as an excellent hostess who frequently entertained large numbers of guests. She read widely, particularly history, philosophy, political economy, and theology. She also read about women's rights; Mary Wollstonecraft's *A Vindication of the Rights of Women* was one of her favorite books. She developed a keen memory and an analytical mind that was capable of independent thought.

As her children grew older and needed less direct attention, she became more active at Quaker meetings. In 1821, she was appointed a minister at the age of twenty-eight. In 1828, when the liberal Hicksites split off from the Orthodox Friends, Lucretia and James Mott faced a difficult decision. Ultimately, after much deliberation, they joined the Hicksites.

Lucretia believed strongly in "inward spiritual grace" and the following of an "inner light." She believed in individual interpretation, not just following fixed creeds or rigid rituals. Her view of religion was based on justice and reason that expressed itself in "practical godliness," that is, it must be lived—not just thought.

Occasionally, James Mott's business suffered a temporary reverse. On one such occasion, Lucretia and her cousin established a school associated with the Quakers' Pine Street Meeting. The school was successful, and the income that Lucretia earned from the school helped the family over its temporary financial difficulty.

## The Antislavery Movement and the Underground Railroad

The decade of the 1830s was a time of reform, and the Quaker community in and around Philadelphia was one of the earliest to participate in antislavery activities. The abolitionist movement was one of the principal opportunities for practical godliness for the Motts. Their home on Arch Street became a station on the Underground Railroad, and they spent considerable time and effort helping escaped slaves.

Lucretia stated clearly her view of the antislavery effort: "I endeavor to put my soul in [the slaves'] stead—and to give all my power and aid in every right effort for their immediate emancipation. The duty was impressed upon me at the time I consecrated myself to the gospel which anoints 'to preach deliverance to the captive, to set at liberty those that are bruised.'"

The Motts not only provided food, clothing, and shelter to fugitive slaves but also risked physical injury. One day, a slave who was running away from his master sought refuge at the Motts' house. He ran into their home, through the parlor, and hid in the rear of the house. James Mott barred the door to the enraged master and "calmly stood at the door with a lighted lamp barring the way. He barely escaped death when the angry master threw a stone ... past his head and it crashed into the side of the door."

On another occasion, former slave Daniel Dangerfield, who had worked for years on a farm near Harrisburg, was brought to trial as a fugitive in Philadelphia. Lucretia rallied

her friends in support of Dangerfield. In court, she sat directly behind the defendant. Edward Hopper, the Motts' son-in-
law, who was the defense attorney for Dangerfield, called on
"witness after witness to testify Dangerfield's long residence
in Pennsylvania." Lucretia spoke with the judge, a fellow
Quaker, during the recess: "I earnestly hope that thy con-
science will not allow thee to send this poor man into
bondage."

After an all-night court session, Dangerfield was acquit-
ted due to a technical error in the writ of accusation involving
his height. Many of the people present at the trial credited
Lucretia with having a major influence on the verdict. One of
the men present observed: "She looked like an angel of light.
As I looked at her, I felt that Christ was here."[46]

On a third occasion, the Motts provided a refuge for Jane
Johnson and her two sons. Jane, a slave belonging to John H.
Wheeler, the U.S. Minister to Nicaragua, was attempting to
take advantage of Pennsylvania's antislavery laws to gain
freedom. William Still, a leader of the Underground Railroad,
and Passmore Williamson, secretary of the Pennsylvania
Anti-Slavery Society helped Jane to escape from her master.
Wheeler took legal action to obtain the return of his slaves.

An indictment was obtained against Williamson and his
associates, who were accused of "conspired effort" to encourage Jane to run away. Lucretia accompanied Jane to the trial,
attended all of the court sessions, and then took Jane to stay
at the Mott home for several days. Lucretia convinced Jane
that she should testify in her own behalf at the trial to show

that she wanted to leave her master. Jane's testimony was a key factor in obtaining her release from bondage.

Williamson's accomplices were found by the jury to be not guilty of kidnapping and rioting charges, but they spent a week in jail for assault and battery because they had to pull Jane away from Wheeler, her master. Passmore spent three months in jail for contempt of court because he told the court that he didn't know where Jane was. Jane and her sons stayed several more days with the Motts and then were guided successfully to Canada and freedom via the Underground Railroad.

In December 1833, the American Anti-Slavery Society was formed in Philadelphia. Lucretia was one of four women invited to attend their first convention, but women were not permitted to join the new organization. They formed the Women's Anti-Slavery Association, and Lucretia was elected president. When a Pennsylvania branch of the national society was established, James Mott was a charter member. Again, Lucretia was not invited to join; however, the rules were changed two years later to allow women members. She became an active, influential member.

**The Women's Rights Movement**
Lucretia Mott was an active supporter of Angelina and Sarah Grimké in their early efforts to speak in public to mixed audiences of men and women. Lucretia gave them advice and encouragement when they were being harassed for attempting to speak in public. Sex discrimination had existed from the

beginning of the antislavery movement, but the prejudice against the Grimkés was more than Lucretia could bear. From this point onward, she was driven by the "women question." She considered it to be "the most important question of my life."

When Lucretia accompanied her husband to London to attend the World Anti-Slavery Convention in 1840, where she met Elizabeth Cady Stanton, she was prepared for rejection as a woman delegate. When she was rejected, being prepared didn't make it any less painful. Lucretia forced the issue of women's participation to the floor of the Convention instead of being handled by the Executive Committee behind closed doors. However, she lost her proposal to let women be active delegates. Lucretia and Elizabeth were relegated to the gallery with the other women to observe the activities of the Convention, not to participate in them.

Instead of sitting quietly in the gallery, Lucretia and Elizabeth toured London while discussing "the propriety of holding a woman's convention." Despite the twenty-two-year differences in their ages, the two women had much in common. Elizabeth looked up to Lucretia, who was more widely read and was more used to active participation in organizations and to public speaking. Lucretia became Elizabeth's mentor. They agreed to convene a meeting to address women's issues when they returned to the United States. They didn't realize it at the time, but that meeting wouldn't occur for another eight years.

Upon their return to Philadelphia, James published *Three*

*Months in Great Britain.* The book displayed his viewpoint as an individual and provided objective comments written in a serious tone. His gravity was a contrast to the writing in Lucretia's journal, which conveyed her incisive wit and her personal opinions on many subjects. James included observations on the natural beauty of the lakes and mountains in Scotland; Lucretia relied on others to tell her that something was worth seeing.

Elizabeth and Henry Stanton stayed in England and Europe for an extended visit, and when they returned home Henry was occupied studying law and Elizabeth was busy raising her young children. Only after the Stantons moved to Seneca Falls after living in Boston did the planning for the meeting about women's rights occur. It was facilitated by Lucretia Mott's attendance at a Quaker meeting in the area and visiting friends and relatives in nearby Auburn.

Lucretia and Elizabeth met at the home of Jane and Richard Hunt in Waterloo. Also present were Lucretia's sister, Martha Wright of Auburn, and Mary Ann M'Clintock, a Quaker abolitionist from Waterloo. At this planning meeting for the Convention, the five women discussed their frustration with the limited rights of women and the discrimination they had experienced in the abolitionist and temperance movements. Elizabeth Cady Stanton was particularly vocal. All five women had attended antislavery and temperance conventions, but Lucretia was the only one with experience as a delegate, orator, and organizer.

They prepared a notice about the first Women's Rights

Convention to be held on July 19-20, 1848, in the Wesleyan Chapel in Seneca Falls. They also agreed to reconvene at the home of Mary Ann and Thomas M'Clintock in Waterloo on July 16 to prepare an agenda for the Convention. At this meeting, Elizabeth Cady Stanton was the principal author of the *Declaration of Sentiments* modeled on the *Declaration of Independence*. The only difference of opinion among the five women was whether or not to include women's right to vote in the *Declaration of Sentiments*. Elizabeth Cady Stanton prevailed, and it was included.

James Mott called the Convention to order. He stood tall and erect, radiating confidence as he presided over the Convention. Lucretia Mott stated the goals of the Convention and discussed the importance of educating women and of improving the standing of women in society. *The Declaration of Sentiments* was discussed and adopted with minor changes. The resolution about the right of women to vote was the only one that wasn't adopted unanimously. Some of the attendees were concerned that pushing the elective franchise might reduce the probability of achieving other goals. The resolution was left in the document.

Lucretia also spoke at the second Women's Rights Convention in Rochester two weeks later. This was a more intellectual audience, and several conservative clergymen quoted St. Paul on the duty of women obeying their husbands: "Man shall be the head of woman." Lucretia was eloquent in response: "Many of the opposers of Women's Rights who bid us to obey the bachelor St. Paul, themselves reject his counsel—he advised them not to marry." These clergymen learned to respect Lucretia's knowledge of the Scriptures.

In 1849, Lucretia prepared a "Discourse on Woman" speech in which she rebutted many of the male speakers' objections to the Women's Rights Movement. She wrote: "Let women then go on—not asking favors, but claiming as a right the removal of all hindrances to her elevation in the scale of being—let her receive encouragement for the proper cultivation of her powers, so that she may enter profitably into the active business of life."

In 1850, Lucretia convinced a Quaker businessman, William Mullen, and his wife to help raise funds to found the Female College of Pennsylvania in Philadelphia. Lucretia and James Mott were also the principal sponsors of the Philadelphia School of Design for Women (now the Moore College of Art). The Motts assisted Pennsylvania's first female attorney to gain admission to the Commonwealth Bar exams. Lucretia believed in doing things, in accomplishing things, not just in talking about them.

In the fall of 1850, Lucretia met women's rights leader Lucy Stone at the First National Women's Rights Convention in Worcester, Massachusetts. The two women became close friends and frequent correspondents. By the end of the following year, Lucy Stone began to devote her energies to the Women's Rights Movement and not to split her efforts between that activity and the abolitionist movement.

Over her objections, Lucretia presided over the National Women's Rights Conventions in 1852 in Syracuse and in

1853 in New York City. The Syracuse Convention proved to be "a stormy and taxing" event at which many verbal attacks were made on Lucretia. Again, her critics at the meeting quoted liberally from the Bible. Lucretia and Antoinette Brown, as an ordained minister, countered these critics. Most reviews in the newspapers referred to the women's "firm and efficient control of the meetings."

The New York City Convention was also a rowdy one. In fact, a mob broke up the Convention on the evening of September 6. The women attendees retained their composure, and Lucretia congratulated them for their "self-reliance" at the meeting on the following morning. Margaret Hope Bacon said of Lucretia that "no one else had the poise and authority to keep order nor the leadership to carry the frightened women through such ordeals."

More rowdies entered the convention hall during the day, interrupted the meetings, and became so unruly that the evening session was adjourned early. At the time of adjournment, "the hall exploded in confusion." Lucretia observed that some of the women were afraid to leave the hall, so she asked her escort to take them out to the street. Lucretia's escort asked how she would get out of the building. Lucretia reached for the arm of the nearest troublemaker and said: "This man will see me through."[47] He was surprised, but he saw her safely through the exit door.

### The Autumn Years

On April 10, 1861, Lucretia and James Mott celebrated their

fiftieth wedding anniversary. Their friends prepared a statement for the celebration: "James and Lucretia Mott, having completed fifty years of married life, we the undersigned, assembled on the tenth day of April, 1861, to celebrate their Golden Wedding, joyfully record here our names in loving and respectful tribute to them who have given to us, and to the world another illustration of the beauty and glory of true marriage."

In May 1866, the American Equal Rights Association was formed in New York to push for the rights of all citizens, without regard for age, class, gender, or race. Lucretia was elected president. She said that she "would be happy to give her name and influence if she could encourage the young and strong to carry on the good work."

James Mott died on January 26, 1868. Lucretia and James were so close and so compatible that she was "numbed" by his passing. She told a friend: "Scarcely a day passes that I do not think, of course for the instant only, that I will consult him about this or that." James was much more than the husband of Lucretia Mott. He was an independent thinker known for the strength of his convictions. He made the decision to leave the Orthodox Friends and join the Hicksites before Lucretia made the same decision.

James Mott was president of the Pennsylvania Anti-Slavery Association for many years and was active in the American Anti-Slavery Society. He was respected as an individual and for his participation in solving the social problems of the nineteenth century. He was elected or appointed to many offices of trust in various reform movements. He had strong beliefs about women's equality with men. As a young man in 1820, he had told his parents that he couldn't understand why the Society of Friends did not give men and women equal power in "meetings of discipline."

Lucretia continued to be active and in 1870 was elected president of the Pennsylvania Peace Society. On April 14, 1875, she was the honored guest at the centennial celebration of the Pennsylvania Abolition Society. Henry Wilson, Vice President of the United States, presented her to gathering: "I ... present to you one of the most venerable and noble of American women, whose voice for forty years has been heard and has tenderly touched many noble hearts. Age has dimmed her eye and weakened her voice, but her heart, like the heart of a wise man and wise woman, is yet young."

In 1878, Lucretia attended the thirtieth anniversary celebration of the first Women's Rights Convention in Seneca Falls. She spoke at the celebration; her speech included the observation: "Give women the privilege of cooperating in making the laws, and there will be harmony without severity, justice without oppression." Frederick Douglass and Belva Lockwood spoke to the gathering on the topics of equal pay for equal work, improved educational opportunities for women, and women's suffrage. Belva Lockwood was the first woman lawyer admitted to practice before the U.S. Supreme Court and the first woman candidate for President of the U.S. who received electoral votes.

On November 11, 1880, Lucretia Coffin Mott died in her

sleep. Several thousand mourners attended her burial at Pairhill Cemetery. A member of the Peace Society made some brief comments on her life and a silence fell over the mourners. Someone asked: "Will no one speak?" Someone replied: "Who can speak? The preacher is dead!"

Lucretia Mott's portrait hangs in the National Gallery in Washington, D.C. Adelaide Johnson's sculpture of Lucretia Mott, Susan B. Anthony, and Elizabeth Cady Stanton stands in the U.S. Capitol. In *Century of Struggle*, Eleanor Flexner cited the relationship of Lucretia Mott to the other principal leaders of the Women's Rights Movement: "Lucy Stone was its most gifted orator ... Mrs. Stanton was its outstanding philosopher ... Susan B. Anthony was its incomparable organizer ... Lucretia Mott typified the moral force of the movement." Lucretia Mott was the senior stateswoman of the Women's Rights Movement and the mentor of its younger members.

# Chapter 9

## MARIE AND PIERRE CURIE

*"Life is not easy for any of us. But what of that. We must have perseverance and above all confidence in ourselves. We must believe that we are gifted for something, and that this thing, at whatever costs, must be attained."*

*Marie Curie*

*"One must make of life a dream, and of that dream a reality."*

*Pierre Curie*

Marie and Pierre Curie are one of the most famous examples of a successful man / woman team. Marie left her native Poland for France because she knew that she had no opportunity for higher education in her native country. She was one of the first women to receive a Ph.D. in France. Pierre provided her with laboratory equipment and space during her early work that led to their discovery of radium. Pierre's initial research was on crystals; he began to work with Marie on radioactive substances when they realized the potential in that area. Both Marie and Pierre were introverts with simple tastes. They spent their honeymoon bicycling through the French countryside. His wedding gift to her was a scientific book.

Marie was an incredibly hard worker, and Pierre was extremely well-organized. In their early work, his reputation as a scientist opened doors for them. When they began to publish, both were given credit for their research. Marie and Pierre were achievers, but they accomplished more as a team than either could have accomplished separately. Pierre was killed when he stepped in front of a horse-drawn carriage while preoccupied reading a paper that he was having published. Marie was devastated; they were extremely close both in their careers and at home with their family. However, she carried on their research and established an international reputation in the scientific community.

## Marie Sklodowska at the Sorbonne

Marie Sklodowska moved from her native Poland to Paris in

1891 to study at the Sorbonne because women weren't permitted to attend college in Poland. She graduated first in her class with a master's degree in physics. She realized that mathematics was important to her career, so she studied for a second advanced degree. Within a year, she graduated second in her class with a master's degree in mathematics.

In 1894, Marie was asked by the Society for the Encouragement of National Industry to prepare a paper on the magnetic properties of various kinds of steel. Her laboratory at the Sorbonne wasn't adequate for the assignment. One of her professors introduced her to the laboratory head of the School of Chemistry and Physics of the City of Paris, which had the necessary facilities. The head of the laboratory was thirty-five-year-old Pierre Curie, who was already a distinguished physicist for his pioneering work on the symmetry of crystals.

## Pierre Curie—Laboratory Head

Pierre and his brother, Jacques, discovered that certain crystals develop an electric charge when compressed. This conversion of mechanical energy to electrical energy is called piezoelectricity. They used this principal to construct an extremely sensitive electrometer that could detect small amounts of electricity.

Pierre discovered that the magnetic properties of substances undergo change at specific temperatures. The formulation of this fact became known as Curie's Law, and the temperature at which the change occurs was named the Curie

Point. Pierre also invented an ultra-sensitive balance scale that could accurately measure weight of small quantities of material. He sold the patent to a chemical firm; he had no desire to profit from the manufacturing of products based on his scientific discoveries.

Pierre was attracted to Marie from the time they met. They had been invited for tea at the home of Professor Kovalski and his wife. In the biography of her mother, *Madame Curie,* Eve Curie describes her parents' first meeting:

> The conversation, at first general, was soon reduced to a scientific dialogue between Pierre Curie and Marie Sklodowska. Marie, with a shade of timidity and deference, asked questions and listened to Pierre's suggestions. He in turn described his plans, and described the phenomena of crystallography which fascinated him and upon which he was now engaged in research. How strange it was the physicist thought to talk to a woman of the work one loves, using technical terms, complicated formulae, and to see that woman, charming and young, become animated, understand, even discuss certain details with an infallible clear-sightedness ... How sweet it was![48]

Pierre's first gift to Marie was his most recent article, "On the Symmetry in Physical Phenomena: Symmetry of an Electric Field and of a Magnetic Field." Marie was the first woman he had met who was totally without coquetry, and who had an interest in science comparable to his interest.

## Early Marriage Years

On July 26, 1895, after a ten-month courtship, Marie and Pierre Curie were married in a civil ceremony. Their honeymoon was a bicycle trip through the French countryside.

Eve Curie describes the early days of her parents' marriage:

> During these happy days was formed one of the finest bonds that ever united man and woman. Two hearts beat together, two bodies were united, and two minds of genius learned to think together. Marie could have married no other man than this great physicist, than this wise and noble man. Pierre could have married no woman other than the fair, tender Polish girl, who could be childish or transcendent within the same few moments; for she was a friend and a wife, a lover and a scientist.[49]

Pierre's workday didn't change measurably after their marriage, other than he now did his research alongside his beloved wife. Marie's already full workday expanded to doing household chores in addition to spending the day in the laboratory. She rose early to go to the market, and she and Pierre shopped at the butcher's or grocer's on the way home from the laboratory. They lived on the 500 francs a month that Pierre earned at the School of Physics. Marie handled their finances.

In August, 1896, Marie placed first in her class in her final examinations for the teaching certificate. Her paper on the magnetic properties of steel was ready to be published. She decided to study for a doctorate in science. Other women had attempted to earn this degree, but, up until that time, none had been successful. Marie would be a pioneer in her next academic effort, and she was acutely aware that she would have to compete with men on their terms. She would have to overcome considerable male prejudice; she didn't hesitate to undertake the challenge.

Both Marie and Pierre wanted children. Their busy lives were made busier during the second year of their marriage when Marie was pregnant with their first child. On September 12, 1897, Irène, a future Nobel prize winner, was born. Marie bathed, dressed, and changed her daughter, but, during the day when she worked at the laboratory, a nurse cared for the baby. Pierre was a loving father, but he let Marie make many of the child-rearing decisions. Their second child, Eve, was born on December 6, 1904.

One of Pierre's main interests continued to be inventing new apparatus. Marie enjoyed their brainstorming sessions in the laboratory with their colleagues. Pierre usually led these sessions while capturing their thoughts at the blackboard in an "atmosphere of peace and contemplation." As a team, their individual strengths complemented each other. Pierre provided many of the creative ideas and the unusual viewpoints to a problem, but it was Marie's perseverance that implemented Pierre's theories and carried them to a meaningful conclusion.

Their home life was quiet. They spent considerable time reading technical journals. Birthday parties were one of their few opportunities to entertain. Marie enjoyed sitting in the garden on Sundays while engaging in technical discussions with their neighbors, who were also colleagues. The children played in the yard under her watchful eye.

## Discovery of Radium

Marie would have to do original work of substance, such as solving a previously unsolved problem or making a discovery that would add to the world's knowledge. The topic for her dissertation evolved from the work on X-rays by Wilhelm Roentgen. His work stimulated Henri Becquerel to investigate whether X-rays were related to the property of fluorescence that causes some crystals to emit electromagnetic radiation, especially of visible light, after being exposed to light.

Becquerel duplicated Roentgen's experiment by exposing fluorescent materials to sunlight and then placing them adjacent to a photographic plate covered with black paper. The first material he found that would fog the photographic plate was a uranium compound (uranium salts). He found that the plates wrapped with black paper became fogged even if they weren't exposed to sunlight. His first conclusion, that the emitted rays were caused by exposure to sunlight, was incorrect. The emitted rays were spontaneous emissions inherent to the crystals themselves. Becquerel found that these emanations came from all uranium compounds.

Marie's subject for her dissertation was to discover the source of these emitted rays. Becquerel had published his findings a year and a half previously. He received little publicity on his work, and no one appeared to be following up on his discovery. Marie had to find a laboratory in which to work. Neither she nor Pierre had sufficient laboratory space, and they couldn't afford to rent a lab for this purpose.

Marie was given an unused storeroom on the grounds of the School of Physics. It was a rough wooden shed with a leaky glass roof and without electricity or heat. In the winter, the temperature inside her makeshift laboratory dropped to forty-two degrees Fahrenheit, which caused her to question some of her results. She had to beg and borrow instruments to equip her laboratory, including some instruments that had been invented by Pierre and his brother, Jacques.

Marie's early results indicated that the strength of the emitted rays was directly proportional to the quantity of uranium in her sample. She could heat the sample, expose it to light, or combine it with other chemicals, but the intensity of the rays remained constant. She concluded that this radiation she was encountering must be a property of the atom of the substance. This critical hypothesis led to the further investigation of the structure of atoms. She examined all known pure chemicals, as well as chemical compounds such as oxides and salts. She found that thorium as well as uranium indicated radioactivity on her electrometer.

She asked Pierre to provide her with samples containing uranium and thorium from the School of Physics. She was surprised to find that three of the samples that Pierre had provided, chalcocite, pitchblende, and uranite, indicated considerably greater radioactivity than the amounts of uranium and thorium in the samples warranted. She repeatedly tested her results. She concluded that there was another radioactive element in the samples in addition to uranium and thorium. It was an element of considerable strength, and it seemed to have the greatest intensity in pitchblende, an ore of uranium.

In April, 1898, Marie announced to the Academy of Science the probable existence of a powerful new element in pitchblende. Her next challenge was to isolate the element, refine it to a pure a substance, and determine its atomic weight. Pierre set aside his other projects to work with Marie in the laboratory. He considered this to be a temporary diversion. He didn't know that their collaboration was to last for the remainder of his life.

They ground the pitchblende ore into smaller particles, boiled it with acids and other chemicals, filtered it, tested both the slush and the residue, and discarded the portion that indicated no radioactivity. Then they repeated the process in an attempt to break down the ore into its component elements. At the conclusion of the process, they found rays emanating from two residual elements, not just one. In July, they announced the existence of a new element similar to bismuth that was 400 times more radioactive than uranium. They named it polonium, after the ancient name for Poland, Polonia.

In December, 1898, Marie and Pierre announced the discovery of radium. Laboratory notebooks show that, up until the end of 1898, their roles in the laboratory were similar. After that time, Marie undertook the daunting task of isolating radium. Pierre concentrated on explaining the phenomenon of radioactivity. Marie worked principally as a chemist; Pierre became primarily a physicist. This division of labor was somewhat dependent on their intellectual strengths. Marie was more practical than her husband, and Pierre was more of an abstract thinker than his wife.

However, they sometimes reversed their roles. Marie was better at abstract mathematics than her husband, and Pierre enjoyed the practical task of designing and building instruments. Referring to the Curie's collaboration, Henri Poincaré, the French mathematician and physicist, observed that their work together involved not only an exchange of ideas, but also "an exchange of energy, a sure remedy for the temporary discouragements faced by every researcher."

Pierre admitted to a friend that, working on his own, he wouldn't have undertaken the task of isolating radium. He said, "I would have gone a different way." Irène Curie observed: "One can discern that it was my mother who had no fear of throwing herself, without personnel, without money, without supplies, with a warehouse for a laboratory, into the daunting task of treating kilos of pitchblende in order to concentrate and isolate radium."

Marie was more concerned than Pierre about the opinion of others about their research. Marie looked for and persuaded others to help them with their work. The diffident Pierre was more willing to concentrate on his work and to ignore the opinion of others, even if they could contribute positively to their efforts.

In 1902, after working almost four years reducing six tons

of pitchblende to its component elements, they had one tenth of a gram of gray-white powder. About one gram of radium can be obtained from seven tons of pitchblende with current reduction processes. Radium has some of the chemical properties of barium, and the intensity of its radioactivity is 900 times that of uranium.

However, Marie and Pierre were confronted with a significant obstacle to further work in the laboratory. They didn't have the funds to obtain the large quantities of pitchblende that were required for future experiments. Radium was present in less than one part per million in pitchblende. They obtained several tons of pitchblende from a mine at Joachimsthal, Northern Bohemia. The uranium had already been extracted for other industrial uses, so their task was made easier. Since the pitchblende was considered waste, they obtained it by paying transportation costs.

They worked in primitive conditions, and their work required long hours of hard, physical labor. Wilhelm Ostwald, a distinguished German chemist, observed: "At my urgent request the Curie laboratory, in which radium was discovered a short time ago, was shown to me ... It was a cross between a stable and a potato-cellar, and, if I had not seen the work-table with the chemical apparatus, I would have thought it a practical joke."

The working conditions were considered by two highly motivated people to be secondary to the content of the work. Marie's views were, " ... it was in this miserable old shed that the best and happiest years of our life were spent entirely consecrated to our work. I sometimes passed the whole day stirring a mass in ebullition, with an iron rod nearly as big as myself. In the evening I was broken with fatigue."

The Curies found that radium could cause bad burns, but that it could retard the growth of tumors, destroy infected cells, and arrest some types of cancer. They published more than thirty technical papers between 1899 and 1904. In 1902, Marie graduated from the University of Paris with the degree of Doctor of Physical Science "tres honorable."

In 1903, the Curies shared the Nobel Prize in physics with Henri Becquerel for their pioneering work in radioactivity. They received many honors, including Pierre's acceptance into the Academy of Science and his appointment as a full professor at the Sorbonne. The French government proposed awarding Pierre the Legion of Honor, but he declined it saying: "Please be so kind to thank the Minister and to inform him that I do not feel the slightest need of being decorated, but that I am in the greatest need of a laboratory." The Nobel Prize money allowed Pierre to devote all of his time to research, instead of dividing his time between research and teaching.

Many people had difficulty understanding the nature of the collaboration between the Curies. A writer for *Nouvelles Illustrées* came close to understanding it: "It would be a mistake to believe that it is because of a feeling of conjugal gallantry that Monsieur Curie wanted to associate his wife with the honor of the discovery. In this household of married scientists ... the woman is not an auxiliary but, with all the strength of the word, a collaborator and often indeed the inspirer of the husband."

A writer using the pseudonym, Diogéne, observed:

> It seems that it was Madame Curie, of Polish origin, who took the initiative in the first research, but for the outside world there is only this unity, Monsieur and Madame Curie. No feminism, no masculinism.... How far we are here from the concept of the woman necessarily alone because she is a scientist, of the man of depth hampered in his work by a companion who is an idle social butterfly! ... the ménage equalized aspirations, maintaining each in his / her place and preventing a tug of war. There is neither Monsieur or Madame Curie ... but Monsieur and Madame Curie, whom the Swedish Academy and humanity is pleased to crown with the same, single prize.[50]

A lofty view of the collaboration of the Curies was described by the writer, Flammarion:

> I see in my imagination, He and She, in the age of dreams, both impoverished but rich in hope and seeking I know not what magic talisman to cure the world of its miseries.... With ardor they mix, in the same crucible, the gold of their hearts, of their science, of their experience; then they throw in, without counting the money which, with great difficulty, they have earned as professors.... They labor in silence, marching, without ever looking back, to conquer the sparkling chimera.... And one day, at the bottom of their crucible—joy intense and

unforgettable—they find the treasure they were searching for.[51]

Marie's and Pierre's happy, fulfilled life together didn't continue for long. On April 19, 1906, Pierre went to a meeting with his publisher. It was raining, and the streets were crowded and slippery. Pierre, who was usually preoccupied, didn't see a horse-drawn wagon coming as he crossed the street. He tried to grasp a harness strap as the horses reared. He fell down, and, briefly, it appeared that he was going to escape injury. He avoided the horse's hooves, but his skull was crushed by the wheels of the wagon.

## Marie Continues Alone

Marie was devastated. She was forty years old and was faced with the decision of what to do with her future. She decided to continue their work alone. Marie wrote in her diary:

> My Pierre, I think of you all the time, my head is bursting with the thought of you, and my reason fails. I can't understand that I have to live without you and that I can't smile at my life's companion. The trees have been in leaf two days now and the garden is beautiful. This morning I was admiring the children in it. I thought how beautiful you would have thought them and that you would have called me to show me that the periwinkles and narcissus were out... [52]

She continued to teach. Andrew Carnegie endowed a number of annual scholarships under her tutelage. In 1911,

Marie was nominated again for the Nobel Prize—for work done since Pierre's death. It was the first time that anyone had received a second Nobel Prize.

Even with the international recognition that she received, Marie continued to be a target for the prejudice against women that existed early in the twentieth century. She accepted a nomination for the French Academy of Science and went through the necessary politicking to win the election. She missed election by two votes. This caused her to re-think her standing with her scientific peers in France and to be more aware that her sex continued to be a barrier to her advancement.

The Sorbonne and the Pasteur Institute established a dual laboratory, one in her name for her work in radioactivity and one in Louis Pasteur's name for biological research. The "Institute of Radium: Pavilion Curie" was opened in 1914. In 1925, she traveled to Warsaw to lay the cornerstone for another research facility, the Radium Institute of Warsaw.

She was diverted from her research during World War I, but continued to be productive. She converted a Renault automobile into a "radiological car" to bring X-ray equipment to the front lines. By the end of the war in 1918, she had equipped twenty mobile X-ray units and had installed X-ray equipment in over 200 locations in hospitals.

Initially, Marie and Pierre weren't aware of many of the hazards of working with radioactive materials. Later, Marie became increasingly aware of the risks to her, personally, in working with these substances. She continued with her research, but realized that some of her physical problems were due to her long-term exposure. She worked in the laboratory until May 1934, when a fever caused her to leave. She was diagnosed with bronchitis and exhaustion and died in July 1934 of pernicious anemia.

Marie and Pierre Curie provide us with stellar examples of role models of teamwork. Their personal relationship and working relationship as well as their perseverance and determination, without question, are worthy of our emulation.

Marie and Pierre Curie
Courtesy American Institute of Physics,
Emilio Segrè Visual Archives

# EPILOGUE

*"We have been saying right along that women and men must work together if we are to bring this world safely into the coming century...."*[53]

*"Moving Beyond Rhetoric" in* Women: Looking Beyond 2000 *by Gertrude Mongella*

What is the environment within which men and women will work together in the future? What can be done to improve our roles in this evolving environment? In *Fire in the Belly: On Being A Man*, Sam Keen offers suggestions for a starting point:

> The healing of the relationship between the sexes will not begin until men and women cease to use their suffering as a justification for their hostility. It serves no useful purpose to argue who suffers most. Before we can begin again together, we must repent separately. In the beginning we need simply to listen to each other's stories, the histories of the wounds. Then we must examine the social-economic-political system that has turned the mystery of man and woman into the alienation between the genders. And, finally, we must grieve together. Only repentance, mourning, and forgiveness will open our hearts to each other and give us the power to begin.[54]

Riane Eisler addresses this alienation between the genders in *The Chalice & the Blade*: *Our History, Our Future*. Eisler describes two distinctly different societies: dominator and partnership. She observes that "the dominator model is what is popularly termed either patriarchy or matriarchy—the ranking of one half of humanity over the other. The second, in which the social relations are primarily based on the principle of linking rather than ranking, may best be described as the partnership model. In this model—beginning with the most fundamental difference in our species, between male and female—diversity is not equated with either inferiority or superiority."

Eisler adds: "If we are ever to have a truly pluralistic society, where people's differences are freely expressed, celebrated—and utilized for everyone's benefit, it must begin with a partnership between women and men." She considers the partnership model to be a "'win-win' rather than 'win-lose' view of power, in psychological terms, a means of advancing one's own development without at the same time having to limit the development of others." She has high expectations for the partnership model:

> The changes in woman-man relations from the present high degree of suspicion and recrimination to more openness and trust will be reflected in our families and communities. There will also be positive repercussions in our national and international policies. Gradually, we will see a decrease in the seemingly endless array of day-to-day problems that now plague us....

> In the world as it will be when women and men live in full partnership, there will, of course, still be families, schools, governments and other social institutions. But like the already emerging institutions of the egalitarian family and the social-action network, the social structures of the future will be based more on linking than ranking. Instead of requiring people to fit into pyramidal hierarchies, these institutions will be heterarchic, allowing for both diversity and flexibility in

decision-making and action. Consequently, the roles of men and women will be far less rigid, allowing the entire human species a maximum of developmental flexibility.[55]

In the partnership society described by Riane Eisler, men and women are thought of as equals. When men and women are considered to be equals, equal pay for equal work is a rational conclusion. Removing the "glass ceiling" is a requirement for creating the partnership society of the future.

The behavior of individuals, teams, and organizations becomes the collective behavior of a society. This change must be a bottom-up change, not a top-down change that is edicted or legislated. The change must come via the individuals who are in a position to hire people, to evaluate job performance, and to establish wages and salaries for specific jobs. Perhaps the change will come when the demand for skilled labor, especially technical labor, dictates equivalent pay for men and women performing the same functions.

Only when men view women as equals and women view men as equals can our world move in the direction of the partnership society. In *The 7 Habits of Highly Effective People*, Stephen R. Covey makes some astute observations about the individuals that will populate the partnership society:

> We obviously value the physical differences between men and women, husbands and wives. But what about the social, mental, and emotional differences? Could these differences not also be the sources of creating new, exciting forms of life—creating an environ-

ment that is truly fulfilling for each person, that nurtures the self-esteem and self-worth of each, that creates opportunities for each to mature into independence and then gradually into interdependence? Could synergy not create a new script for the next generation—one that is geared to service and contribution, and is less protective, less adversarial, less selfish; one that is more open, more trusting, more giving, and is less defensive, protective, and political; one that is more loving, more caring, and is less possessive and judgmental?[56]

Covey discusses some of the potential improvements in the environment in which the man / woman teams of the future will strive. He provides us with some desirable goals and a hopeful scenario for the third millennium. Plans and goals are extremely important. However, plans must be implemented and goals must be achieved in order to affect change. The best way to deal with change is to become change agents ourselves.

# TEAMWORK

## (As practiced by world-champion and olympic-champion ice dancers Jayne Torvill and Christopher Dean)

"At the heart of the relationship is trust. It grew from the earliest days of working together, from our own commitment and reliability, tried and tested time and time again ... For the present and immediate future, the commitment ... is total....

Trust is the foundation. But in practice, the relationship has its complexities and conflicts. Chris is a strict timekeeper, whatever the circumstances ... Jayne is the relaxed one. She'll never be early if she can help it.

Jayne is annoyed by Chris's niggling. We'll be coming off the ice after a good performance, usually with Chris leading, and Jayne will hear him say over his shoulder: 'I don't know about this step, or such-and-such a lift.' Niggle, Niggle, there's always something. She dismisses the remark with 'Mm, yeah, sure.' Or if he insists: 'Can't stop. Got to change.' Or she pretends she never heard.

But these are routine annoyances. They have no effect on the underlying trust, or on the qualities that make the relationship work.... Instinctively, automatically, we support each other. If anyone else dares to accuse Chris of being undiplomatic, Jayne cuts in with, 'What do you mean he shouldn't have said it? He was cross! Why shouldn't he say it?'

We complement each other. If Chris is the creative force, never satisfied with what we've achieved, always pushing for more, needing more, *kneading* more, Jayne is the clay, moulding herself to his ideas, understanding the aims, responding, and interpreting.

After all the years together, we have built up a shorthand way of working. Chris will say something like, 'Lay into me, back inside-outside edge.' It might mean nothing to another skater, but she'll know it and do it. He's the artist, sketching a vision in words; she sees it and makes it instant reality ...

While he follows a train of thought, suggesting and coaching, she watches and remembers.

That's the role she's happy with. She never wanted to be the leader, she'd rather stay in the background and deal with whatever comes at her. Any expressions of impatience from Chris—and there are a few sometimes after hours of work on steps that don't come out right—bounce right off her. Close friends call her 'the Rock.'

Emotionally, that's how it works. But physically, when we are together on the ice, the roles are often reversed. If you add up how many turns Jayne has, you would see that she is often the more active one, Chris the rock.

But it is not that she merely does what she's told or ignores him when it suits her. Often, she rules from behind. She responds to the music as much as he does, and if she disagrees with something, if she feels that it really is not going to work, she can see why, and thinks, 'If I do that, I won't be able to get out of it elegantly.' Then she tells him, and shows him.

'See, it won't work.'

'Oh, right.'

Sometimes, the exchange happens so quickly that anyone else would miss the glance between us. Often, in anything concerned with skating, we know each other's reactions at once. When we talk, it's usually about skating, and we constantly interrupt each other to finish of each other's thoughts....

We stay together only by sticking to a self-disciplined regime. The rules are quite simple and very demanding. Commitment, hard work, attention to detail. Those are the elements that focus us."[57]

From *Torvill & Dean: The Autobiography of Ice Dancing's Greatest Stars* by Jayne Torvill and Christopher Dean

# NOTES

*"We are foolish, and without excuse foolish, in speaking of the superiority of one sex to the other, as if they could be compared in similar things! Each has what the other has not; each completes the other; ... and the happiness and perfection of both depend on the each asking and receiving from the other what the other can only give."*

*John Ruskin*

## Preface

1 Keen, Sam. *Fire in the Belly: On Being A Man.* (New York: Bantam, 1991) 208, 214.

## Chapter 1

2 Zolotow, Maurice. *Stagestruck: The Romance of Alfred Lunt and Lynn Fontanne.* (New York: Harcourt, Brace & World, 1965) 6.

3 Zolotow, Maurice. *Stagestruck: The Romance of Alfred Lunt and Lynn Fontanne.* (New York: Harcourt, Brace & World, 1965) 117.

4 Zolotow, Maurice. *Stagestruck: The Romance of Alfred Lunt and Lynn Fontanne.* (New York: Harcourt, Brace & World, 1965) 30.

5 Zolotow, Maurice. *Stagestruck: The Romance of Alfred Lunt and Lynn Fontanne.* (New York: Harcourt, Brace & World, 1965) 70.

6 Brown, Jared. *The Fabulous Lunts.* (New York: Atheneum, 1986) 393.

7 Brown, Jared. *The Fabulous Lunts.* (New York: Atheneum, 1986) 393-394.

8 Zolotow, Maurice. *Stagestruck: The Romance of Alfred Lunt and Lynn Fontanne.* (New York: Harcourt, Brace & World, 1965) 172.

9 Brown, Jared. *The Fabulous Lunts.* (New York: Atheneum, 1986) 396-397.

## Chapter 2

10 Lyon, Peter. "The Antic Arts: Two Minds That Beat As One." *Holiday.* 30 December 1961. 149.

11 Lyon, Peter. "The Antic Arts: Two Minds That Beat As One." *Holiday.* 30 December 1961. 149-150.

12 Comden, Betty. *Off Stage.* (New York: Simon & Schuster, 1995) 134-135.

13 Kasha, Al and Joel Hirschhorn. *Notes on Broadway.* (Chicago: Contemporary, 1985) 73.

14 Comden, Betty and Adolph Green. *Singin' in the Rain: Story and Screenplay.* (London: Lorrimer, 1986) x.

## Chapter 3

15 Burns, George. *Gracie: A Love Story.* (New York: G.P. Putnam's Sons, 1988) 15.

16 Burns, George. *Gracie: A Love Story.* (New York: G.P. Putnam's Sons, 1988) 14.

17 Burns, George. *Gracie: A Love Story.* (New York: G.P. Putnam's Sons, 1988) 78.

18 Burns, George, with Cynthia Hobart Lindsay. *I Love Her,*

*That's Why!* (New York: Simon and Schuster, 1955) 153.

19 Burns, George, with Cynthia Hobart Lindsay. *I Love Her, That's Why!* (New York: Simon and Schuster, 1955) 156.

20 Burns, George. *Gracie: A Love Story.* (New York: G.P. Putnam's Sons, 1988) 227-228.

21 Burns, George. *Gracie: A Love Story.* (New York: G.P. Putnam's Sons, 1988) 228-229.


**Chapter 4**

22 Gilbreth, Frank, Jr., and Ernestine Gilbreth Carey. *Cheaper by the Dozen.* (New York: Thomas Y. Crowell, 1948) 1-2.

23 Gilbreth, Frank B. *Motion Study, A Method for Increasing the Efficiency of the Workman.* (New York: D. Van Nostrand, 1911) v.

24 Gilbreth, Frank B. and L.M. *Applied Motion Study.* (New York: Sturgis & Walton, 1917) xi.

25 Yost, Edna. *Frank and Lillian Gilbreth: Partners for Life.* (New Brunswick: Rutgers UP, 1949) vii-viii.

26 Yost, Edna. *Frank and Lillian Gilbreth: Partners for Life.* (New Brunswick: Rutgers UP, 1949) 125.

27 Yost, Edna. *Frank and Lillian Gilbreth: Partners for Life.* (New Brunswick: Rutgers UP, 1949) 127.

28 Yost, Edna. *Frank and Lillian Gilbreth: Partners for Life.* (New Brunswick: Rutgers UP, 1949) 130.

29 Yost, Edna. *Frank and Lillian Gilbreth: Partners for Life.* (New Brunswick: Rutgers UP, 1949) 177-178.

## Chapter 5

30 Tisdall, E. E. P. *Queen Victoria's Private Life*. (New York: John Day, 1961) 24.

31 Duff, David. *Victoria and Albert*. (New York: Taplinger, 1972) 225.

32 Thompson, Dorothy. *Queen Victoria: The Woman, the Monarchy, and the People*. (New York: Pantheon, 1990) 44.


## Chapter 6

33 Markus, Julia. *Dared and Done: The Marriage of Elizabeth Barrett and Robert Browning*. (New York: Alfred A. Knopf, 1995) 211.

34 Forster, Margaret. *Elizabeth Barrett Browning: A Biography*. (New York: Doubleday, 1988) 359.

35 Meynal, Alice. "Elizabeth Barrett Browning." *Encyclopaedia Britannica*, vol. 4 (Chicago: William Benton, 1957) 275.

36 Stephen, Leslie. "Robert Browning." *Encyclopaedia Britannica*, vol. 4 (Chicago: William Benton, 1957) 279.


## Chapter 7

37 Kerr, Laura. *Lady in the Pulpit*. (New York: Woman's Press, 1951) 53.

38 Cazden, Elizabeth. *Antoinette Brown Blackwell: A Biography*. (Old Westbury, NY: Feminist Press, 1983) 31.

39 Cazden, Elizabeth. *Antoinette Brown Blackwell: A Biography*. (Old Westbury, NY: Feminist Press, 1983) 87.

40 Cazden, Elizabeth. *Antoinette Brown Blackwell: A*

*Biography.* (Old Westbury, NY: Feminist Press, 1983) 98.

41 Cazden, Elizabeth. *Antoinette Brown Blackwell: A Biography.* (Old Westbury, NY: Feminist Press, 1983) 163.

42 Cazden, Elizabeth. *Antoinette Brown Blackwell: A Biography.* (Old Westbury, NY: Feminist Press, 1983) 165.

43 Cazden, Elizabeth. *Antoinette Brown Blackwell: A Biography.* (Old Westbury, NY: Feminist Press, 1983) 195.

44 Cazden, Elizabeth. *Antoinette Brown Blackwell: A Biography.* (Old Westbury, NY: Feminist Press, 1983) 252.

## Chapter 8

45 Stoneburner, Carol and John, eds. *The Influence of Quaker Women On American History: Biographical Studies.* (Lewiston / Queenston, Ontario: Edwin Mellen Press, 1986) 206.

46 Bryant, Jennifer Fisher. *Lucretia Mott: A Guiding Light.* (Grand Rapids, Eerdmans, 1996) 144-146.

47 Bacon, Margaret Hope. *Valiant Friend: The Life of Lucretia Mott.* (New York: Walker, 1980) 5.

## Chapter 9

48 Curie, Eve. *Madame Curie: A Biography.* (Garden City, NY: Garden City Publishing, 1940) 122.

49 Curie, Eve. *Madame Curie: A Biography.* (Garden City,

NY: Garden City Publishing, 1940) 141.

50 Quinn, Susan, *Marie Curie: A Life.* (New York: Simon & Schuster, 1955) 194.

51 Quinn, Susan, *Marie Curie: A Life.* (New York: Simon & Schuster, 1955) 195.

52 Keller, Mollie. *Marie Curie.* (New York: Franklin Watts, 1982) 71.

**Epilogue**

53 Mongella, Gertrude. "Moving Beyond Rhetoric." *Women: Looking Beyond 2000.* (New York: United Nations, 1995) 122.

54 Keen, Sam. *Fire in the Belly: On Being A Man.* (New York: Bantam, 1991) 211.

55 Eisler, Riane. *The Chalice & the Blade: Our History, Our Future.* (San Francisco: Harper & Row, 1987) 199-200.

56 Covey, Stephen R. *The 7 Habits of Highly Successful People.* (New York: Simon & Schuster, 1989) 263.

**Teamwork**

57 Torvill, Jayne, and Christopher Dean, with John Man. *Torvill & Dean: The Autobiography of Ice Dancing's Greatest Stars.* (Secaucus, NJ: Carol Publishing, 1996) 126, 128-132.

# BIBLIOGRAPHY

Bacon, Margaret Hope. *Valiant Friend: The Life of Lucretia Mott*. New York: Walker, 1980.

—. "Lucretia Mott: Holy Obedience and Human Liberation." *The Influence of Quaker Women on American History: Biographical Studies*. Lewiston / Queenston, Ontario: Edwin Mellen, 1986.

Brown, Jared. *The Fabulous Lunts: A Biography of Alfred Lunt and Lynn Fontanne*. New York: Atheneum, 1986.

Bryant, Jennifer Fisher. *Lucretia Mott: A Guiding Light*. Grand Rapids, Michigan: William B. Eerdmans, 1996.

Burns, George. *Gracie: A Love Story*. New York: G.P. Putnam's Sons, 1988.

Burns, George, with Cynthia Hobart Lindsay. *I Love Her, That's Why!* New York: Simon and Schuster, 1955.

Burton, Humphrey. *Leonard Bernstein*. New York: Doubleday, 1994.

Casper, Joseph Andrew. *Stanley Donen*. Metuchen, New Jersey: Scarecrow, 1983.

Cazden, Elizabeth. *Antoinette Brown Blackwell: A Biography*. Old Westbury, NY: Feminist Press, 1983.

Comden, Betty. *Off Stage*. New York: Simon & Schuster, 1995.

Comden, Betty, and Adolph Green. *Singin' in the Rain: Story and Screenplay*. London: Lorrimer, 1986.

Covey, Stephen R. *The 7 Habits of Highly Effective People*. New York: Simon & Schuster, 1989.

Cromwell, Otelia. *Lucretia Mott*. Cambridge: Harvard UP, 1958.

Curie, Eve. *Madame Curie: A Biography*. Garden City, New York: Garden City Publishing, 1940.

Curie, Marie. *Pierre Curie*. New York: Macmillan, 1932.

Cutter, Rebecca. *When Opposites Attract: Right Brain / Left Brain Relationships and How To Make Them Work*. New York: Dutton, 1994.

Duff, David, *Victoria and Albert*. New York: Taplinger, 1972.

Eisler, Riane. *The Chalice & the Blade: Our History, Our Future*. San Francisco: Harper & Row, 1987.

Eyck, Frank. *The Prince Consort: A Political Biography*. Boston: Houghton Mifflin, 1959.

Forster, Margaret. *Elizabeth Barrett Browning: A Biography*. New York: Doubleday, 1988.

Gilbreth, Frank B. *Motion Study, A Method For Increasing the Efficiency of the Workman*. New York: D. Van Nostrand, 1911.

Gilbreth, Frank B. and L. M. *Applied Motion Study*. New York: Sturgis & Walton, 1917.

Gilbreth, Frank B., Jr., and Ernestine Gilbreth Carey. *Cheaper by the Dozen*. New York: Thomas Y. Crowell, 1948.

Graham, Maureen. "Lucretia Mott: 1793-1880." *Women of Power and Presence*. Wallingford, PA: Pendle, 1990.

Green, Stanley. *The World of Musical Comedy*. San Diego: A. S. Barnes, 1980.

Hallowell, Anna Davis, ed. *James and Lucretia Mott: Life and Letters*. Boston: Houghton Mifflin, 1884.

Hare, Lloyd C. M. *The Greatest American Woman: Lucretia Mott*. New York: American Historical Society, 1937.

Hays, Elinor Rice. *Those Extraordinary Blackwells: The Story of a Journey to a Better World*. New York: Harcourt, Brace & World, 1967.

Hewlett, Dorothy. *Elizabeth Barrett Browning: A Life*. New York: Alfred A. Knopf, 1952.

Hirschhorn, Clive. *Gene Kelly: A Biography*. London: W. H. Allen, 1974.

Jenkins, Anne Elizabeth. "Lucretia Mott." *Heroines of Modern Religion*. Freeport, NY: Books for Libraries Press, 1970.

Karlin, Daniel. *The Courtship of Robert Browning and Elizabeth Barrett*. Oxford: Clarendon, 1985.

Kasha, Al and Joel Hirschorn. *Notes on Broadway: Conversations with the Great Songwriters*. Chicago: Contemporary, 1985.

Keen, Sam. *Fire in the Belly: On Being A Man*. New York: Bantam, 1991.

Keller, Mollie. *Marie Curie*. New York: Franklin Watts, 1982.

Kerr, Laura. *Lady in the Pulpit*. New York: Woman's Press, 1951.

Longford, Elizabeth. *Queen Victoria: Born to Succeed*. New York: Harper & Row, 1964.

Lyon, Peter. "The Antic Arts: Two Minds That Beat As One." *Holiday*. 30 December 1961: 149+.

McCormack, James Patton. *As a Flame Springs: The Romance of Robert and Elizabeth Barrett Browning*.

New York: Charles Scribner's Sons, 1940.

Markus, Julia. *Dared and Done: The Marriage of Elizabeth Barrett and Robert Browning.* New York: Alfred A. Knopf, 1995.

Meynal, Alice. "Elizabeth Barret Browning." *Encyclopaedia Britannica*, vol. 4. Chicago: William Benton, 1957.

Mongella, Gertrude. "Moving Beyond Rhetoric." *Women: Looking Beyond 2000.* New York: United Nations, 1995.

Quinn, Susan. *Marie Curie: A Life.* New York: Simon & Schuster, 1955.

Reid, Robert. *Marie Curie.* New York: New American Library, 1975.

Robinson, Alice M. *Betty Comden and Adolph Green: A Bio-Bibliography.* Westport, CT: Greenwood, 1994.

Shearman, Deirdre. *Queen Victoria.* New York: Chelsea House, 1986.

Stack, V. E. *How Do I Love Thee? The Love-Letters of Robert Browning and Elizabeth Barrett.* New York: G. P. Putnam's Sons, 1969.

Stephen, Leslie. "Robert Browing." *Encyclopaedia Britannica*, vol. 4. Chicago: William Benton, 1957.

Sterling, Dorothy. *Lucretia Mott: Gentle Warrior.* Garden City, NY: Doubleday, 1964.

Stoneburner, Carol and John, eds. *The Influence of Quaker Women on American History: Biographical Studies.* Lewiston / Queenston, Ontario: Edwin Mellen Press, 1986.

Taplin, Gardner B. *The Life of Elizabeth Barrett Browning.*

New Haven: Yale UP, 1957.

Thomas, Donald. *Robert Browning: A Life Within Life*. London: Weidenfeld and Nicolson, 1982.

Thompson, Dorothy. *Queen Victoria: The Woman, the Monarchy, and the People*. New York: Pantheon, 1990.

Tisdall, E. E. P. *Queen Victoria's Private Life: 1837-1901*. New York: John Day, 1961.

Torvill, Jayne, and Christopher Dean, with John Man. *Torvill & Dean: The Autobiography of Ice Dancing's Greatest Stars*. Secaucus, NJ: Carol Publishing, 1996.

Winwar, Frances. *The Immortal Lovers: Elizabeth Barrett and Robert Browning*. New York: Harper & Brothers, 1950.

Woodham-Smith, Cecil. *Queen Victoria: From her Birth to the Death of the Prince Consort*. New York: Alfred A. Knopf, 1972.

Yost, Edna. *Frank and Lillian Gilbreth*. New Brunswick, NJ: Rutgers UP, 1949.

Zolotow, Maurice. *Stagestruck: The Romance of Alfred Lunt and Lynn Fontanne*. New York: Harcourt, Brace & World, 1965.

# INDEX